Tales of a Multifaceted Life

Volume 3

By Enice Toussaint

Éditions Nouveau Siècle

Éditions Nouveau Siècle

The "Nouveau Siècle (ENS)" editing house proposes heartfelt and personal works where freedom of expression comes first. In this day and age, despite all the conflicts, we are experiencing a world that is more unified. This is in large part due to telecommunications and a borderless global economy. This new form of reality facilitates exchanges between cultures and the conceptualization of a human identity finally in harmony with itself.

It is within such a vision of peace that this editing house intends to promote its activities: Publishing personal words, born of individual experience, wanting to testify to a world in transformation To charge ahead into this new century, we must go forth without fear of change, of difference, of being yourself, of your thoughts and the thoughts of others. With such a philosophy, true words, even the simplest ones, can help to nurture renewal within our world.

"Nouveau Siècle's" Mission Statement: To share thoughts and preserve memories…

Publisher: Éditions Nouveau Siècle ENS

Email adresse ediontionsens@gmail.com

Webite: : www.enspublishing.com

Project manager:

Natatsha Casimir

Book cover's conception:

Natatsha, Elle-Camay C. Reason, and Max Casimir

Computer graphics of cover page: Elle-Camay C. Reason

Photography, Makeup: Natatsha Casimir

Conception of the website: Audio Publishing

© 2001, Éditions Nouveau Siècle and Enice Toussaint

© 2004, Éditions Nouveau Siècle and Enice Toussaint for the translation into English,

Copyright

Éditions Nouveau Siècle ENS and Enice Toussaint

All rights reserved

ISBN: 978-1-80623-724-1 - Print
ISBN: 978-1-80623-723-4 - e-book

Handling in 2nd trimester 2025 Copyright

Bibliothèque Nationale du Québec

National Library of Canada -e-book

In memory of my mother. For my children n Natatsha and Max, who helped me realize this writing project. To my grandchildren, whom I adore. May they cherish the memory of each life and thus learn perseverance.

Your life can be filled with joys and satisfactions. We cannot allow obstacles to destroy well-being and happiness. We are defeated only if we accept defeat.

Martin Gray

The Book of Life

Table of Contents

Chapter 1 1
    An evocation of the past 2
    My evocation continues. 4
    A stay in New York 7
    At my sister's house, on Mentana Street 9

Chapter 2 14
    Our house on Laval Street in Le Plateau-Mont-Royal 14
    Description of the house in Laval, September 1995 14
    Our life on Laval Street (Plateau-Mont-Royal) 18
    And what should happen 27
    Natatsha's Birth 29
    Christmas 1995 in Laval Street 33
    Chronicle of a fall... Imminent 33
    Jacques' approach to a return to life as a couple 36
    Preparations for our departure for Haiti 41
    Heading for Haiti 41

Part Seven 46
Our departure for Haiti, stopover in New York 46

Chapter 3 49
    My Life in Haiti with Jacques, 1996 49
    An unbearable ordeal 52
    I continue my story. 56
    Miragoâne from the 1990s to the present day 57
    The first steps in Haiti 58
    The second stage of our experience in Haiti 65

At my niece Yolaine's house 65
The Sorry Cayenne Experience (1996) 75
Our stay in Miragoâne, June 1996 80
The feast of Saint-Jean-Baptiste 80
Preparing for my return to Montreal 83
A look back 90

Chapter 4 93
A solo return to Montreal. 93
Back with My Kids 1996 93
Another stay in Haiti 98
A second cover with Jacques. 98
The aftermath of Jacques' operation in Haiti 109
A Christmas Night Under the Stars, 1996 122

Chapter 5 125
Emergency return to Montreal, Thursday, December 26, 1997 125
Jacques ends up at Notre-Dame Hospital 125
In the hospital: back to my story 127
Retrospective of the progress 133
The operation of Jacques' arm 134

Chapter 6 140
Life together on Port-Royal Street 140
Living with James in a 2 1/2 140

Chapter 7 145
Among the nuns 145
My stay with the nuns 145
I continue my story 149

Chapter 1

The day after my deliverance from Jacques.

Part One

The day after I left home, I started writing again. As proof, here is what I had written down.

Journal — June 6, 1995
I have left Jacques

I left Jacques on June 6, 1995 at 11:45 a.m., as well as my son Max. I had $60 in my pocket to rent a moving truck and pay for gas.

After 19 years of living together with Jacques, I can say that I left naked, with only my pride and dignity. I know that God will help me get out of this: he is so generous, this God.

I decided to lead my life differently. I become another Enice. The first little Enice stayed in the mirror at Jacques' and I hope she never comes out again.

I'm going to make a promise: I, the new Enice, decide to take charge of my life, to take care of my health from now on and to forget the suffering I've endured for 27 years, which began with my first husband Tony. (End of the newspaper)

An evocation of the past

The evening I left Jacques, I went to Vivianne's and stayed for three days. The first night, I had a lot of nightmares, but I still managed to sleep. I felt liberated and at peace. Vivianne was very kind to me, as well as her daughters, Marlene and Marie.

In one of my dreams, I saw a man who looked like the unknown lover who was rocking me with the sweetness of his eyes and his smile. I was like in a sweet mirage, I felt good. For nothing in the world would I have escaped from this dream: I am certain that this man was my guardian angel. I was woken up by the ringing of the phone. Vivianne was next to me because I had laid down in her bed.

She informed me that Jacques was on the phone, that he wanted to talk to me, and that he wanted her to wake me up. I told Vivianne to answer him that I would call him back; She hung up. My message having been conveyed, she hung up. She wanted to know the reason for the call. I then revealed to him what Jacques had said the day before.

The day before, he had asked me to come early the next morning to file the accounting files, because an agent would come and check them; I also had to explain how to do the accounts. Vivianne immediately said to me: "What do you mean, you've just left home, he already wants to see you again! But who does he think he is? Calmly, I began to reassure Vivianne.

Around 10 a.m., the phone rang again. It was Jacques again, this time in a very bad mood. He shouted at me: "What time are you coming?" and I replied: "No, I don't come; if you want, call me for another appointment, and if I come, Max must be available, because I don't want to meet you without the presence of a third person. He told me, "I order you to come right away". I immediately hung up.

Vivianne exclaimed: "You answered well, bravo!"! Then she smiled. I spent two beautiful days at her house. She made me laugh continuously. We went for long walks. Since there was a bakery near her house, we went there several times to buy warm bread. We were also going shopping.

I felt like a bird that had regained its freedom after spending years in a cage. After three days, I went to live with my sister with Max. Aunt Dédia had invited me to go and spend two weeks with her. She assured me that staying there would take my mind off things and that Jacques would leave me at peace. For at least a few days. I accepted. Before I left, I had arranged a meeting with him, but in the company of Max, for Saturday, June 10.

My Diary

Saturday, June 10, 1995

I'm at my sister's house. She and my brother Robert are very nice to me, and they spoiled me a lot. We are happy. I am quite sure that my mother in the afterlife is happy about it, as is my father. (End of the newspaper)

My evocation continues.

I had made an appointment with Jacques to update the company's accounts, while Max was supposed to help him tidy up the yard. It was for June 10.

As agreed, on Saturday morning of June 10th, we left early because Max had to report to work in the evening. That morning, my heart was sad. I didn't feel any desire to see Jacques. I was scared, and my hands were sweaty. Max has noticed this. While driving the car, he shook my hand. I understood his gesture, and in any case, he didn't want to go either, but he didn't express his state of mind.

When we arrived, I immediately headed to the office to start work. Max stayed with Jacques in the courtyard. I was in a hurry so that I could finish everything before Max left for work. Jacques was kind to us. Max and I finished at the same time, but I had to provide him with details of all the processing I had done in the company's files. Max, for his part, could not linger any longer. As for me, I was leaving for New York the following day, while the auditor was coming in three days. While assuring me that the rest of our interview would be quite brief, Jacques expressed the desire to discuss the future of the company with me. "Don't worry, you can go, I won't hurt your mother," he promises Max.

Max immediately asked me if I would agree to stay. I said yes, but only for 15 minutes. He left, not very reassuring. For my part, I was clearly on the defensive.

I tried to explain everything to Jacques. I had filed the files in a very orderly way, according to weeks, months, and years. He returned to the question of the future of the company. He wanted me to continue to work with him so that we would not lose the government grant.

I let him talk for a few minutes, then I stood up and replied: "Listen to me, Jacques, I don't want to work with you anymore and we are no longer associates. For the subsidy, I won't go to the appointment, you can go alone. I'm sure you'll get it because I had designed a good business plan for you. He begged me. I remained adamant and walked to the door. He held me back with force.

He told me that he wanted to talk to me about the future of our relationship and my upcoming trip to New York. I let him know that I was just going to New York to think about it. He asked me if he was going to separate or divorce. I was about to answer, but he cut me off, saying, "I'll tell you one thing, if I'm going to live with you, you'd have to eliminate your sister Irene and your daughter Natasha from your life." At the time, Elle-Camay had not yet been born. After giving me this ultimatum, the pig wanted to make love to me. I pushed him away with a good punch, then I took the way out. While he was pitifully trying to apologize, I told him that it was too late to rebuild our relationship. Back at my sister's house, I told my family what had happened.

Martine, Jacques' sister, had come from New York with her ex-husband to visit me. My sister had invited them to dinner. I told them about some incidents that had happened with Jacques.

As Martine was due to return to New York on June 11, I suggested that we make the trip together. Here are the details of this trip recorded in my travel diary.

A stay in New York

June 12, 1995

I arrived in New York at 7:15 a.m. Aunt Dadia and her daughter Aldine had picked me up at the bus station. As soon as I arrived at their house, even before lunch, I went to bed. I slept until 2 p.m.

I spent seven wonderful days in New York City with Aunt Dadia and her family. They helped me a lot morally; they have made me regain my self-confidence; They took me to places I had never visited before. With her two daughters, Aldine and Delia, Aunt Dadia took me shopping; they bought gifts for Max for his graduation. This suited me perfectly since I was thus exempted from making these expenses myself. One of the girls asked me to point out to Max that it was the first time she had dressed a man; She was very proud of it. On June 21, I left for Montreal with a racing heart.
4 p.m. I take a break.

End of the break.

4:20 p.m. *I had made a short stop to stretch my legs. I walked down the hallway for ten minutes. Through the window, I* *admired the beautiful sun warming nature, and the leaves falling. Despite the sun, the temperature was quite cold.*

Today, I write with a very calm mind; I feel really good. I have freed myself from him and feel a sense of softness.

I admit that all is not over; I feel that I still have a lot of things to change internally. I will continue my writing activity with much more enthusiasm. It's really wonderful, what I'm feeling right now.

Part Two

At my sister's house, on Mentana Street

At my sister's house, it was very good. She had a large bedroom that had two beds, but she and I slept together. Max slept in a small bed in the living room. My brother's room was at the back of the house. It had a large terrace in the courtyard. In fact, the cover of my book, *one woman among many others*, represents this court. At the back, two large garages, whose entrances overlook the alley. We were, all things considered, very well settled.

Back in Montreal, I called my doctor to get an appointment. Since New York, I haven't felt well. I couldn't concentrate and I couldn't stop sweating, I felt anxious, and I felt nervous, excrement. My sister, my brother, Vivianne, my children, and my friends joined forces to try to make me happy. I was surrounded and pampered.

Jacques called me frequently, but I refused to speak to him. Finally, my sister let him know that he should not call her house anymore. He agonized her with insults. My sister hung up on him. Since then, he has never called again. I no longer felt the slightest feeling for him.

When I met with my doctor, he asked me what had happened in my life. I told him the story of my separation from Jacques. He felt that it would be better for me and that everything would be fine for my health from now on. I must point out that while I was living with Jacques, he was my family doctor; but at the same time, he was my therapist. When I went to see him, I took up nearly an hour of his time to tell him about my sorrows, as well as the psychological, physical, and sexual wickedness that Jacques inflicted on me. I was still crying when I left his office. I was mostly relieved. He gave me confidence. He prescribed antidepressants at that time, while recommending that I not abuse them. Since my blood pressure was high and I had a point in my heart, he sent me for an electrocardiogram.

Immediately, I started taking my medication, and I felt better. It was a miracle. I started going out with my sister very often.

I had a wonderful summer. Natatsha often came to see me. Her belly had begun to become rounder. Max had found a small contract related to his job as a draftsman. His girlfriend came frequently to visit him.

My sister's house was a duplex. She had rented the upstairs apartment to someone named Jean. He was an interior decorator.

Since he had a friend who was an architect, it was through him that Max had obtained the contract from this friend. Jean was not only Irene's tenant, but he was also a friend of the family.

He organized small parties at his house; Occasionally, I would go with my sister. She liked to receive her friends at her home and offer them good food. She always made too much, but it didn't cause any problems: since there were always friends coming over, she gave them the surplus. She justified herself by reminding me that she was imitating my mother, who always prepared much more food than expected. She was still convinced that someone was going to come through. At the end of the evening, there was indeed nothing left.

My sister loved to share. Like our mother. I share, too, but I don't like to cook. At the time I lived with Jacques, cooking had become too demanding. It took away my taste for preparing food.

In the meantime, a very unpleasant problem had arisen and was growing. Even though he continued to live in the house, Jacques refused to pay off the debts: telephone, electricity, mortgage, etc. It turns out that, unfortunately, the telephone and electricity costs were in my name. The house was still very badly maintained and bearably dirty.

For the electricity and telephone bills, I had finally managed to have my name removed, but I still had to pay the arrears. I was able to negotiate agreements to pay for everything at my own pace. At the same time, I received an income supplement. So, things were looking good for me on the financial side. My sister had helped me reduce the amounts on my credit cards. In short, at the end of the month, I had fewer payments to make.

By July, Max had started working full-time. I took the opportunity to explain to my sister that, since my son would need more privacy, we were planning to rent an apartment together. This would allow us to share the costs. She recognized that it was a very good idea.

When I started looking at the classifieds for an apartment, my sister offered to go and do a whole thing with her on the Plateau, so we would immediately notice signs for renting apartments. I immediately liked the idea.

As we were looking for the signs that said "For Rent," my sister said, "Let's also look to see if there are any houses for sale." I replied, "It's going to be a long time before I buy a house; I'm not saying no, but not for the moment, we'll see for later. She told me to let her do it. "How?" I replied. That's when she made me this proposal: "If I buy an income house, you and Max can live on the ground floor; with a tenant on the first floor, the house itself will be able. With your rent money, I will pay the mortgage. »

I spoke about it shortly afterwards with Max, who was delighted with the idea. We found a house located on Laval Street between Rachel and Duluth. A ten-minute walk from my sister's house.

The house was quickly purchased. There was the floor to be redone, as well as the painting and repairs of lesser importance. Our friend Dédé and my son have combined their efforts to execute them. My sister took me to buy furniture, because I had left most of my furniture at Jacques'. We bought a living room set, a four-poster bed, a writing desk, and a chair. The oven and the fridge, and everything else, I already had them.

The house was well-appointed. For the bed, I had made muslin curtains and other curtains for the windows on the ground floor and those in the basement. Max's room was very large. He had bought a beautiful set of bedrooms at Brault et Martineau, including a queen-size bed.

About this house, I would like to give you a description as precise as possible. We entered it in September 1995.

Chapter 2

Part One

Our house on Laval Street in Le Plateau-Mont-Royal

Description of the house in Laval, September 1995

Our property on Laval Street was a semi-detached duplex. There was an alley at the back where you could drive or walk. It consisted of a basement, a ground floor, and an upper floor. There is also a fairly spacious courtyard, including a magnetic part that was used for parking, as well as a gate. For the moment, I didn't have a car, even though Max's had been scrapped for several months. The upper apartment was rented to a young couple without children.

Max and I occupied the two lower floors. The ground floor had three bedrooms, a large living room, a dining room, a large kitchen, and Max's large bedroom at the back. The basement had a rear exit, a laundry room, a storeroom, a toilet, two bedrooms, and a living room.

We were actually well settled, and everything was going very well. Natatsha came to see us very often. I must point out that I did not have a washing machine. I had warned Jacques that as soon as I had my own home, I would come and take back the washing machine that I had left him temporarily.

As agreed, I called him. I told him that I was going to rent a van to transport the aircraft. He offered to bring it to me himself. I talked to Max about it, and he agreed.

I gave him my address, but told him to call me before coming because he would have to go through the back door. I made sure that Max would be home then. On the scheduled day, he brought the washer and, with Max's help, took it down to the basement. Once the device was installed, Jacques quickly understood that we had the whole house. I claimed that we were the tenants. I didn't offer to visit her.

A few days later, he called me to tell me that he knew that my sister had bought me a house. He immediately began to reproach me. I reacted calmly: "You know, when you're calm, we'll talk about it again." And I hung up the phone.

The incident disturbed me somewhat, because obviously there had been a leak. I have resolved to confide in only members of my close family. Shortly after, one of Jacques' clients called me to inform me that he had left the house to rent an apartment. "According to Jacques' intention," he added, "if your sister bought you a house, he will stop paying the mortgage on hers, unless you go back to living with him." While trying to keep my cool, I told this client that Jacques had stopped paying the mortgage debt a long time ago and that, in any case, I would never go back to live with him. I added that the house where I lived was not mine, that it belonged to my sister, that my son and I were tenants of the apartment downstairs, and that we paid rent and electricity every month. He promised to pass on the message to my ex-spouse and wished me good luck for the future.

I felt quite worried. Without further ado, I asked Max to accompany me for a brief check of the house that had just been abandoned. When we arrived, I was amazed to see the repulsive dirt he had in the house. It was literally a dump. He had left, leaving the headboard, the living room, and the small dining room. I gave the headboard to my daughter; Max sold the living room for $50 to a friend of his who was moving into an apartment. We tried to replace the belongings, pick up what was lying around, and put it in garbage bags. Various metal bars have been stored in a corner of the courtyard. Our neighbour told us that City employees had come to inquire about the owner's new address.

He advised us to place the garbage bags next to the barrier, in anticipation of the garbage truck's passage. Max, for his part, gave me this alert: "Mammy, know that Jacques is not done with you. He's going to do more bad things to you. He warned me to remain vigilant.

Part Two

Our life on Laval Street (Plateau-Mont-Royal)

I remember that we took possession of the house on Laval Street at the end of September 1995. Everything was going very well. I liked the neighborhood, you could find everything there. I also had access to two churches: Saint-Jean-Baptiste on Rachel Street, at the corner of Drolet, and Saint-Jude on Saint-Denis Street, at the corner of Duluth. Many shops lined the rue Saint-Laurent. I used to walk a lot. It allowed me to free my mind.

Every first day of the month, my sister, son, and I would get together to deal with the rent. Since I managed my budget well, I didn't have any money problems, and neither did Max.

I hadn't yet set out to decorate the house. One day, my sister took me to an antique shop to buy some decorative items. I bought a centerpiece, candlesticks, an antique lamp for my nightstand, and a painting. These are memories that I have kept for a long time. Max finally got the painting, Natatsha the centerpiece, and I the small lamp, the only memory I have so far kept of my personal belongings.

My sister was very good to me and my children. Since she worked at the Sainte-Jeanne-d'Arc hospital, she often came to my house and came to dined with me. I would then take her back to her work while taking the opportunity to go for a walk. Every day she came to see me; however, she found something that was not in the right place. I didn't react verbally, but I replaced my emotions in my own way. The next day, she came back to the subject: "Why did you move this table (or armchair)?" Over time, his attitude became irritating and even pained me. But, in order not to offend her, I continued not to reply.

Jacques, on the other hand, was still harassing me. He was watching me everywhere. He wanted me to resume life as a couple with him. I tried to explain to him that we could be friends, but no more. He told me that if he couldn't be my husband, he wouldn't accept being my friend. I retorted that I agreed with him. I was very serious, I didn't feel anything for this man anymore.

But to counter his stubbornness, I didn't know what to do anymore, and I obviously needed psychological help. At times, I felt like something was bursting in my chest. I had started to lose sleep. Sometimes, to sleep, I took two sleeping pills. This lump in my chest was causing me excruciating pain. I was so preoccupied with my problems that I didn't even notice that my health was failing. I often went to church to ask God to come to my rescue.

One day at the Saint-Jean-Baptiste church, I found a pamphlet about a small organization, the Centre du, located in the basement of the church and whose entrance was on Drolet Street. I called: they were nuns of the Sisters of the Good Shepherd.

I went to meet them. They first put me through an evaluation, and then the director told me that she was going to put me in group therapy with Sister Monique. The next day, October 26, 1995, I started my therapy. I went there twice a week. After a week, Sister Monique told me that starting the following week, I would be in individual therapy.

It was one hour, two days a week. On the first day, Sister Monique asked me to tell her about my childhood. I watched it for a few seconds without saying anything. She insisted, "Yes, I'm listening." I was thinking. She kept asking me questions, "Do you have a mother, father, sisters, or brothers? Did you live with your parents? Start with this. Or, if you prefer, tell me about a time in your life when you felt happy. »

I opted for my life as a child, before my mother died. It was quite an experience because I had never really looked back on my previous life, on my childhood; I never had the time to do it.

When I started talking about my childhood, I felt happy. I didn't even see Sister Monique anymore; I was in another world, in my past. I saw all the places and all the people I had known. Sister Monique did not interrupt me. But at the stage of my mother's illness, I stopped. I couldn't go on, I didn't want to go on. She asked me what was going on inside me. I told him that I didn't feel well, that I was too tired. She wanted to discuss it a little more, but I couldn't.

It was not yet time to leave, but I told Sister Monique that I was leaving and that I would come back another time. I left upset, but at the same time, a little more relieved to have talked a little about my childhood. I didn't tell anyone anything about what had happened in therapy. It was my secret, and it was private.

In the meantime, I should help Natatsha prepare her baby's trousseau. We went to buy fabrics to make sheets, curtains, and everything she needed for the child's arrival. We organized everything together.

A while had passed, and suddenly, Jacques started these little games again, which made my stress resurface. I slept badly. I had a terrible nightmare on October 28th.

Here is what I wrote about it in my journal.

October 28, 1995

I woke up at 5 a.m. because I had a dream that stressed me out a lot. In this dream, I was with Jacques, and I was doing many things that made me anxious and tired. When I opened my eyes, I had palpitations.

At the time, I decided to write a letter to Jacques about everything he had claimed about his love for me. I confirmed that our relationship would remain as it was and recommended that she begin therapy. (End of the newspaper).

And here is Jacques' answer: "I will not go to therapy, because I am my own therapist." I continued my therapy at the Center. The nuns offered me to volunteer. I accepted. I went to the centre two or three times a week from ten o'clock to noon. I worked as a receptionist. It was good for me to take my mind off things. As the days went by, I took a painting class with the sisters. I discovered that I had a talent for it.

As far as my therapy is concerned, I ended up crossing the border where I was stuck every time I had to talk about my mother's death, an extremely difficult moment to relive. Since his death, I have never looked back on that time in my life. Let's just say I didn't want to go back.

When my mother left this world, I was nine years old, and I remember that I hardly cried. When I unravelled this mystery in therapy, I cried throughout the session. After that, I felt relieved. I had a good evening at home with my son and sister. I was in a good mood. I would like to point out that I continued to visit the Centre for two years, from 1995 to 1997. During this time, there were two stops. At the same time, I had my daughter, whom I had to take care of. She needed me to take her to the doctor, and I would then help her at home when her husband, Patrick, was working. So, I was very busy. I didn't have time to pay attention to Jacques' whims.

Max made me think that I should put our old house up for sale so that I could pay back Irene and the finance company. I thought it was a good idea. I knew that in order to sell the house, I would have had to finish the work that Jacques had never finished. I also knew that he wouldn't have wanted to do them, and I didn't have the money to hire professionals to do it. Max and Irene said that Jacques had broken the house, so it was up to him to arrange the renovations. I agreed, I had done too much; it was his turn now. But I knew that Jacques was clever, though, I was going to talk to him about it anyway.

When I told him about it, he agreed that we should put the house up for sale. I explained to him that before putting it up for sale, he had to finish the renovations he had started. He told me that he would only do the renovations of the house if I agreed to help him. Otherwise, no renovation. I let him know that I needed time to think about this.

I talked to my sister and Max about it, and the latter told me that he will sometimes come with me to work, but he doesn't have tools! So, it was Jacques who had them. So, I called Jacques, and I informed him that I would help him, and that Max was going to accompany me, and that day he touched me or made indecent gestures, I would not go anymore. He agreed with my terms.

He worked at another location while we met at home in the afternoons, at least 3 days a week, until the work was done. At first, I went by bus, but after a while, he offered to pick me up from home. He was nice to Max and me.

Some time later, he gave me a small car that one of these customers was selling. He wanted to buy it for me, but I knew him too well not to accept his offer. When I told Irene and Max about it, they told me to take as much as I could from him, because you've done a lot for him. This time, he was very careful of me, and was doing things a little outside of his usual character. He did things to please me. Despite that, I was always on my guard.

Sometimes he would invite me to a restaurant, and my son thought it was a sign that he had changed. Still, I never invited him to our house, and I didn't go to his house either. When we worked together in the house, he respected me and he kept his word not to touch me. It seems that he was a different man than the Jacques I knew. Despite all his gestures, I couldn't trust him. My heart remained closed. I didn't want to suffer again. (Here is what I wrote in my diary on November 1st and 2nd).

November 1, 1995 — Journal

I went to pick up Patrick's car from work, so I could go out with Natatsha. We went to see her doctor. Everything is fine, the baby is doing well, the cervix is dilated by one centimeter. That being said, we went to do some shopping. Around 3:30 p.m., we went to pick up Patrick from work. They dropped me off at my house. After preparing dinner, I started sewing the bedding for the baby's arrival. At a certain point, I was too exhausted to continue, I went to bed.

November 2, 1995 — Journal

Today, I had an appointment at the women's center for 3 p.m., I sent it back for next time. This morning, I woke up at 8 a.m. Vivianne called me to let me know that she is coming to my house. Jacques also called me to ask me what time I would be at the little house. I told him that I would be there around 6 p.m. After talking to them, I went back to sleep and woke up at 9:30 a.m. I had a nice coffee and breakfast.

Max had a noon appointment with a gentleman. This morning, I wasn't in good shape. I still felt exhausted. it was noon, and I wasn't dressed yet. At around 12:15 p.m., Vivianne and the man arrived at the same time, under a torrential rain. Vivianne was soaked.

The center called me to ask if I could come back tomorrow morning to help them, and I agreed. Although I wasn't in great shape, I knew I was going to be better the next day, and it also felt good to go.

I was delighted that Vivianne had come. I made another good coffee and went to take my shower very quickly. Afterwards, I invited Vivianne to my room so that we could talk while getting dressed. Afterwards, we had dinner, talked about everything and nothing, and watched the show "Young and the Restless." Vivianne left around 3 p.m. I wanted to take a nap before going to work with Jacques at home, but I couldn't because I was too tired to sleep. That afternoon, I went to work because I wanted to achieve my goal, to finish the renovation of the house. It was important to me. I know that if I don't go to help Jacques with the house, he won't be either. So I sacrificed myself to get there. I know that God will help me. (End of the newspaper).

I was exhausted, I always had a lot of things to do, but it was the right tiredness. To help my health, I started taking vitamins. Vivianne came to see me when I had time, and we had fun together.

Diary
November 15, 1995

I haven't written since November 2nd; I was too busy with the work of the house on Boyer Street. And I should help my daughter prepare for her delivery.
On Friday, November 10th, Natatsha had a contraction, and we took her to the hospital at 2 a.m. False alarm, we came home at 9 a.m. on Saturday.
On Sunday, November 11, at noon, we returned to the hospital, another false alarm. (End of the newspaper).

And what should happen

I was continuing the repair work with Jacques in the house, but one evening, when we had finished work, he shot at me. He squeezed me so hard that I couldn't get away. He wanted to kiss me, but I didn't want to, so I squeezed my mouth. He started to rip off my clothes, and I was struggling, but he ended up raping me. I couldn't scream. There was no one there. I felt like vomiting.

Since I didn't have a car, I left the house on foot and took the subway to go home. The same evening, he called me, but I didn't answer, so he left a message apologizing. When I called him back, I told him that it was better to leave work after the holidays, and also, I would be busy helping my daughter. He agreed with my decision.

Part Three

Natatsha's Birth

After the false alarms, I brought Natatsha to our house, That way, she would be safe, and I wouldn't need to go back and forth. Patrick stayed in the apartment every afternoon, and he came to spend the evening with us. I went to my sister's house less often. I was taking care of my daughter, and Jacques didn't call me too often, as I had told him to leave me at peace. I had the impression that he was preparing for another episode.

Natatsha and Patrick were discussing the name of their baby. Natatsha didn't want him to have Patrick's last name, and it stressed him out. To clarify, I told them that the baby and their future children could have both their names. Patrick agreed with me.

A week after the false alarm of November 10, we went to see her gynecologist. I explained to him how I had problems when I had my children. After examining my daughter, she informed us that she would have to wait another two weeks. I told him about the possibility of a caesarean section. She told me that she was able to deliver her child without having a caesarean section.

When we got home, she went to see Patrick in the hospital, because he would have to have surgery for the gallbladder; he had had a liver attack, and he had to go to the hospital urgently. When she returned, Natatsha complained of fatigue. She told me tonight that she wouldn't go to see Patrick in the hospital. The next day, Sunday, I prepared a bath for her and helped her into it. I was worried about her. I found that her face had changed and so had her color. It was as if swollen.

She told me that she wanted to walk to the church of Saint-Jure and afterwards, she would like to go to my sister's house. I called my sister to tell her not to bring the food to our house because after church, Natatsha and I were going to come to her house. I added that the idea came from my daughter, not from me. She begged me to be careful.

It was late afternoon. When we arrived at Irene's house, we ate. My sister told me that it was better if Natatsha was taken to the hospital because she didn't like her condition. I agreed with her.

Since the hospital wasn't too far away, we walked through Lafontaine Park and arrived. It was December 2nd, and we went for a simple exam. We wanted him to watch the movements of the baby's heart. The nurse immediately put her in the specialized room for the examination. She noticed that the child was hardly moving and that the heart was slowed down. She rang the emergency bell to call the chief medical officer, who had arrived two minutes after her call.

The surgeon examined Natatsha and informed us that the cervix had not dilated. He said a few minutes later that the baby would have died if he had not been taken away. At the same time, he called his doctor. He spoke to the doctor sternly. He told her, "This lady should have had a caesarean section a long time ago"! He was not satisfied with the gynecologist's work.

In the meantime, I called Patrick's mother, who was at her son's bedside in the hospital; he had just had surgery. I told him not to reveal anything to his son. However, I explained everything to him. She promised me that she would jump in a taxi to keep Natatsha company as well.

When she arrived, Natatsha was already in the operating room. Half an hour later, the nurse brought us a pretty little girl with eyes wide open, and a fully formed face that moved; one would even have thought that she was smiling. We gave each other a hug; we skipped the three together and burst with joy, and thanked God.

I took the child in my arms and I repeated, "Thank you, Jesus!" I forgot that Patrick and Irene's mother were there and that they were waiting for their turn to take our pretty little girl in their arms. The nurse also informed us that Natatsha is doing well and that she will be discharged in a few minutes. We were preoccupied with our little miracle girl.

My daughter had always thought that she would give birth to a boy. Natatsha was taken to the room. She was half awake. I introduced her to her daughter and said, "Look at your beautiful little girl!" She opened her eyes and whispered, "A girl, what do you mean, a girl?" and then she fell asleep. When she woke up, she was very happy with her little baby.

Patrick's mother (Gerda) stayed with my sister and me until the wee hours of the morning. We left Natatsha with the baby in the hospital, and Gerda came to sleep at my house. The next morning, she went to the Sainte-Jeanne-d'Arc hospital to see her son and tell him the good news. She couldn't have done it the day before because he had just had surgery and wasn't fully awake.

The next day, I also went to the hospital early to see my daughter. She stayed there for nearly eight days in the hospital because she had a temperature. I went to St. Jude's Church to thank

God, St. Jude, and the other saints for saving my children. At any rate, I had almost lost them; Thanks to my vigilance, they survived.

When they came back from the hospital, Natatsha and Patrick and their new baby came to my house because they couldn't take care of the baby themselves, because of their condition because of their health.

A week later, it was better. But I was completely exhausted. They stayed at home for a month. Before they left, my daughter gave me a big bouquet of flowers to thank me.

Part Four

Christmas 1995 in Laval Street
Chronicle of a fall... Imminent

During the holiday season, Natatsha and Patrick, and their daughter were still at my house. I went to Irene's less and less to Irene's. She came to see us. She thought that my house was a mess and that I let the children change my place. I always claimed that I was the one responsible for all this disturbance. She was really not happy.

Every New Year's Day, Irene receives all the family and friends at her home. My daughter and I had decided to organize a small party on the evening of December 25th.

The children had the opportunity to invite their friends and relatives. Natatsha invited only one friend. She has never had many friends, and that has been the case until now. For my part, I had invited Vivianne and her daughters as well as my sister, but she didn't come. A few days before, Jacques had come to see his daughter and the baby. He had brought an envelope containing a small amount as a gift for the child, so he intended to redeem himself. He had come to reconcile with Natatsha and Patrick. He asked me if I would go for a coffee with him, because he had things to tell me. I accepted, and he told me that he had things to tell me. Even then, I didn't invite him to the party. He encouraged me to think by emphasizing that he wanted to resume living together with me. He swore to me that he was not the same man, that he had changed entirely.

Jacques started to keep calling me to see if I was ready to start again with him. He called me constantly, and some days, every hour of the day. He urgently wanted to check if I was finally willing to reconcile our couple.

Finally, I talked to the children about it. They felt that he had indeed changed and that I should give him a second chance. The night before New Year's Day, we went out together, and he took me home. He forced me to have sex with him, but my heart ached. Every time he tried to make love to me, I felt sick. I had the painful impression that I was betraying myself.

First of all, I didn't refuse to have sex with him, and I wanted to vomit every time. I saw again all the miseries he had inflicted on me, and I also saw his betrayals. I didn't feel anything for him anymore. I suffered in silence, but he finally convinced me. He took advantage of my vulnerability to seduce me and drag me into his trap.

Back to the present
6:15 p.m. I go downstairs to supper.

7:15 p.m. When I come back from dinner, I pack my bags again because I'm leaving tomorrow at 5 p.m. Tomorrow, I want to spend the day writing. I won't have time to devote to suitcases, and above all, I don't want to be stressed. I'm satisfied with my work. I achieved the goal I set for myself. I'll come back and take another two weeks to complete my task, or I'll try to continue at home. At least the first volume is finished, and I've started the second. I arrived in the year 1995. During my time here, I wrote about 17 years of my past, from 1978 to 1995. I think that tomorrow, I will arrive at 1996. I'm happy and proud of myself. Thank you to Jesus.

Part Five
Jacques' approach to a return to life as a couple

After Christmas, a few days before New Year's Day, I called Jacques, but he was away. I called him back on his cell phone, and he signaled what he had to do before New Year's Day.

In the meantime, I had accepted the small Rabbit car that he had given me. On December 31, I decided to go and pay him a surprise visit. I had planned that if he wasn't home, I would wait for him to come back outside.

When I arrived, I rang the bell; No one answered. I took advantage of the fact that someone was opening the front door of the building to sneak me in. I figured that Jacques might be working in the garage. I walked over and saw his van. As I was going up the stairs, I noticed a red car coming in; the person who was driving it was Jacques. He had a young lady next to him. I left the building immediately. I wanted to avoid him seeing me.

I immediately got back in my car, getting ready to leave, when Jacques came knocking on the window of my vehicle. he wanted to talk to me. I ignored him and quickly emptied the place. When I got home, I heard the phone ringing. It was him. He claimed that he had promised the woman and her children that he would pick them up in Toronto and take them to the December 31 ball. I hung up the phone. I couldn't listen to him anymore. I felt betrayed once again. He continued to call me, and I did not call him back.

After the holidays, he continued his harassment. After several refusals, I finally accepted. I told him that I wouldn't come back to live with him because I didn't trust him anymore. He suggested that if I agreed to go back with him, it would be better if we moved to another country. He cited Philadelphia and Haiti, emphasizing his preference for Haiti. But in my opinion, Philadelphia would be a better choice, that we could buy damaged houses, renovate them and resell them or rent them. He found all kinds of arguments to favor Haiti. I asked him how much money he planned to use to go and live in Haiti. He blurted out, "With your money that you put in trust." I didn't think at all about the money I had invested for my retirement. Jacques continued, "You don't even know if you're going to live long enough to have that money." I pointed out to him that if I touched that investment, I would lose a lot in percentage interest. He replied that it was not a big deal, and that at least I would have my money in hand. I promised him that I would think about it.

I was obviously ignorant. I never thought that he was interested in my money first. I talked to my children about it, and they asked me if I was really willing to withdraw the money. I convinced them that it was a good deal. Jacques had persuaded me that it was for our good and that we were going to be happy together in Haiti. When I told them that I wanted to go to Philadelphia instead, they recognized that it was a better idea than going back to Haiti.

I talked to Jacques about my preference for Philadelphia, but he didn't want to know anything. Before I gave him my definitive answer and agreed to take the money out of the bank, he treated me with great care.

I finally took all the money in trust and put it in a checking account. The operation turned out to be very expensive. Jacques then took steps to take steps to take action.

I was embarrassed to have to tell my sister whom I had taken back with Jacques. I wrote him a letter to inform him of this. One day, I went to her house and told her that I had written to her to tell her that I had reconciled with Jacques, that I was going to live with him in Haiti. I told her that she had nothing to fear for the house: Max was going to rent the three empty rooms to friends, very reliable young people who worked and whom he knew very well.

She reacted with insults. I didn't fight back because I knew she was right. But, at the same time, I was hardly aware of what was happening, I was like in a black hole. I didn't see the bright side of things. I was like a person with depression. To be noted: I was always thinking of going far away. Even in therapy, I kept repeating this wish. Sister Monique had tried to enlighten me. She had warned me about Jacques, but since I had started to bring him in again, I was always looking for excuses to dodge my therapy sessions. When Sister Monique called me, I said Natatsha needed me. One day, she pointed out to me that my daughter was very familiar with my state of psychological fragility. "Give me the phone, I'll call him." I objected that my daughter did not have a telephone. She then concluded. "I'll be there if you need me, don't forget to call me."

Back to the present

9 p.m.: I approached the window. I was talking to my sister on the phone. I looked out the window. I saw a boat sailing on the river. With its lights on, it was beautiful. It looked like a walking Christmas tree.

Saturday, October 28, 2006

9:30 a.m. I just came back from lunch. I went to the chapel to say a last prayer before returning to Montreal. I thanked God for allowing me to enjoy a good stay here, in this atmosphere of peace. If I isolated myself to write these slices of my life, it's because I wanted to be all alone; I wanted to draw from within myself to put it in order. At the same time, I wanted to find serenity and inner calm. I think I'll really find them again, and I'm looking forward to it.

A friend remarked to me, "I don't think it was necessary for you to isolate yourself to write." I replied: "You know my friend, what I was looking for in myself, I have found it again: an inner peace and I am happy about it." I take the 2 p.m. bus. I arrived in Montreal around 5 p.m.

Part Six

Preparations for our departure for Haiti
Heading for Haiti

Before we started packing our belongings, Jacques and I gleaned information about the conditions of container transport. We booked a 40-foot container. We had two weeks to gather our personal belongings, such as Jacques' tools, furniture, clothes, cars, etc.

We were given 10 days to load the container. So, we had very little time to prepare everything. It was stressful. Jacques had to gather his personal belongings, and I mine, even though we did not live in the same apartment. In addition, some of his personal belongings were in Toronto, which he had not initially told me.

The container was scheduled to be loaded on a Monday. The Friday before, Jacques told me that he had to go to Toronto to pick up these belongings. However, we had in principle finished packing everything. I had bought many boxes, pieces of wood that would work as supports for vehicles, etc. I advised him that he had no choice but to make a quick trip there and back.

So he left on a Friday. No news from Saturday. I then called him on his cell phone, but he didn't answer. I was worried.

During the afternoon, I asked Max to try to reach him at this lady's house in Toronto. He did so and indicated that he wanted to speak to his father. Jacques immediately picked up the phone, he asked me not to worry. Everything was fine, and he would be back that evening. I hung up. I couldn't believe what had just happened. In the middle of the night, my phone rang. That's him. He just wants to let me know that he's on his way home.

When he arrived, he justified himself: "You know, I had to get rid of her gently. These people are so clingy. I asked him if he was sure he wasn't with her anymore. Otherwise, I would cancel everything. He swore to me that he didn't. He was calm and affectionate towards me. However, I was gripped by doubt, and I felt the presence of a barrier between him and me. My heart was no longer his. This departure was going to be an adventure. I was in the waves. That evening, I slept at his house anyway, because we had to go and check on Monday morning if the people in charge had deposited the container at the place planned, in the Saint-Michel district.

We had 8 days to put everything in place. We weren't the only customers. But most of the containers had been rented by traders who were quite used to loading operations. Our container seemed huge to me, and I suggested that Jacques seek the advice of others. He told me that he knew how to do it. "OK, boss," I whispered.

He set about installing a first load. A fellow human being approached him. After introducing himself, he told Jacques that he was doing it wrong. The latter seemed surprised, "Don't take a lot of things on board immediately," his interlocutor first said. You need to get strong wooden plates and planks to stabilize the vehicles. Install the first car; then prepare another floor for the second.

Everything must be strictly compacted. Avoid leaving any gaps so that not even a flat ruler can slip in. You see, my brother, when they arrived in Haiti, all the effects would be mixed. Like a real broth! The man continued, "Imagine a half-filled bottle of fruit. You turn it upside down. All the fruits rise to the surface or remain on top. A word of advice: hire someone experienced to help you. Otherwise, you won't be able to do it alone, and you won't finish loading the entire container on time.

Jacques stared at the stranger with a serious air: "As for the woods, the separation and the like," he admitted, "I agree with you. But to load the container, I'll do it on my own. The man blurted out, "OK, boss," and walked away.

When Max had some free time, he would travel with Jacques and help with the loading. Comrades from his work and his little cousin gave them a hand.

Towards the end, the curious gentleman came back to talk to him and asked him to carry some personal belongings for him to Haiti. He then helped him finish loading the container. During the last few trips, Jacques tried to take everything that was left in the garage and in the yard of the house on Boyer Street. But he did not succeed. He finally left the yard in a great state of disorder. On the last day, they came to pick up the container and brought it on the boat, leaving for Haiti

We had been informed that the crossing would last two weeks. This gave us enough time to prepare for our trip to Haiti.

Back to the present
Return to Montreal

11:50 a.m*. I stop writing. At 12 noon, I go to dinner. When I return to my room, I will no longer write. I have to go back to Montreal. I am very happy with my stay. I leave with peace in my heart. I look forward to seeing my children and their respective spouses, as well as my grandchildren. I am also looking forward to meeting my sister, brother, and close friends.*

I feel like I'm animated by another version of Enice. A more confident and happier version.

Present moment
Montreal
Wednesday, 8 November 2006

10 p.m. Since my return to Montreal on October 29, 2006, I haven't written, not because I haven't had inspiration, far from it. Ideas take shape, they jostle in my head with a crazy desire to go out. The fact remains that I am not yet willing, I have personal matters to solve, which prevent me from continuing.

This time, I decided not to isolate myself to write this part of my life. I am in my room, sitting in front of my secretary who faces the window. I listen to good, inspiring, and peaceful music while writing.

Part Seven
Our departure for Haiti, stopover in New York

The containers gone, we took a week off for the final preparations for our trip. Since the plane tickets were not very expensive, we took advantage of going through New York.

In the meantime, Jacques and I stayed in our respective homes. I packed my bags. I took the opportunity to remind Max to pay my bills in Montreal and make sure that the rooms were rented before I left. In short, everything was well planned.

Two days before we left for New York, Jacques made this suggestion to me: "As a precaution, in order not to run out of money, you should pawn all your jewels." At the time, I hesitated. He then added that when I came back, I would be able to get them back and that, if necessary, the children would go and get them for me.

Again, I listened to him. I pawned everything. I had two pieces of jewelry left that I didn't want to risk: my wedding ring and the bracelet my son had given me as a souvenir of getting his first job. Jacques insisted that I pawn them, too. I couldn't keep anything. I was then forced to buy so-called synthetic jewelry in order to wear it.

Well, you can imagine, I lost everything, like everything else. When I returned from Haiti, I tried to get them back, but a month too late. The pawn shop told me that he had sold them and that there was nothing more I could do. This announcement caused me immense pain. I was revolted. This was all the more so since I realized that all these sacrifices had been useless, and given the painful circumstances of my stay in Haiti with Jacques. I shall never have those jewels again; They remain irreplaceable. In my eyes, they represented an inestimable sentimental value.

Of course, I should have trusted my intuition. But I didn't listen to her. I was then in complete confusion. I couldn't see anything clearly, and I didn't listen to anyone but Jacques. He acted with me in a way he had never done before: attentive, affectionate, respectful. He completely bamboozled me.

After hiring my jewelry, we left for New York. By coach. We stayed for two days in the American economic metropolis, the time to buy plane tickets and get ready to leave.

Several members of my New York family tried to convince me to cancel the trip. Especially Aunt Dadia. I didn't listen to anyone. I falsely but sincerely believed that they did not hold my happiness. Aunt Dadia drove us on March 11, 1996, to Kennedy Airport, where we flew to Haiti.

Chapter 3
My Life in Haiti with Jacques, 1996

My uncle Giordani had to pick us up at the airport in Port-au-Prince. He brought us to his house, which is 15 minutes from the airport.

His wife, Ella, seemed to be waiting impatiently for us, as well as his 7-year-old son. She welcomed us with extreme enthusiasm. The court boy was unloading our luggage from my uncle's van. He carried them upstairs to the room reserved for us. For a few minutes, we gave my uncle and his wife news of the family living abroad. Ella coated our room. I noticed that she provided us with the room that overlooked the street with a balcony around it. It was spacious and airy, well ventilated.

The house had four bedrooms and a toilet on the upper floor, on the first floor, there was a fifth bedroom, a kitchen, a toilet, and a dining room. A wide gallery goes around the house, well framed with wrought iron.

Outside, just in front of the house, a small shop is run by Ella. Two driveways on either side of the shop with two large gates. Without the backyard, the property had two rooms, one for the maid and the little maid, and the other for the court boy and the little servant. Finally, latrines, a kitchen, and the water cistern.

The big drawback was that the street was very busy with cars and trucks during the day and in the evening. The result was a constant noise and a permanent accumulation of dust.

We settled in. Ella came a little later to pick us up for dinner. From my first night, I didn't feel comfortable. I slept quite badly. Jacques made love to me quickly, after which he fell asleep. Unlike him, I stayed awake for a long time. I was worried, without knowing why. I ended up falling asleep. At 5 a.m., our immediate neighbor turned on his radio at maximum volume. Traffic began on the street, with the sound of trucks and cars honking incessantly. With all the noise, I couldn't sleep. I woke up to go and sit on the porch. I was thinking about my children. And I wondered if it was a good idea to come and live here, and if I would be able to hold on for a long time.

As our cars were not yet at customs, we asked my uncle to lend us his van to go there and check if the container had arrived. After getting caught in a traffic jam, we finally arrived at customs. To our relief, the container was there. All we had to do was clear it. Well, it was hell from the beginning.

We spent three days going back and forth to customs. We went there every morning, from 8 a.m. to 4 p.m., without results. Jacques was venting his frustration on me. He was shouting at me in the presence of complete strangers, and he had become very insolent towards me again. On the second day, I decided that I would not go back with him again; he would just have to fend for himself. That day, I started writing again to record a few facts.

April 1, 1996
Newspaper

I'd like to write today, but I'm having a hard time because I have so many things in my head, and the noise of cars and trucks prevents me from concentrating. Jacques went downtown to clear our belongings. He will remain there all day; I didn't go, because he's really despicable with me. He hardly speaks to me, deciding that he has nothing to say to me. I don't understand him anymore: in Montreal, he was sick of me, he was kind, he called me every night to tell me that he loved me, that he couldn't live without me, etc. Since we have been in Haiti, he is a different man. He is arrogant; he only thinks about himself. I thought we were going to have a quiet life, but that's not what happened at all. He even told me that I had become a burden to him.

An unbearable ordeal

I must confess that once again my resolution was short-lived. Shortly afterwards, I agreed to accompany Jacques again to the Haitian customs.

We finally managed to access the container. Three of them went to inspect and check its contents in order to set the fee we had to pay. We then had to hire five customs employees; Jacques' sister and the court boy also came to help us.

We spent a whole day in the blazing sun unloading the container to transfer the belongings to another, while opening each box according to customs instructions. It was oppressively hot. After the audit, we had to grease the inspectors' paws to get a reduction in the fees. And pay the five clerks. When I got home, I was completely exhausted

Two days later, we returned to complete the customs clearance. At the same time, we had to keep an eye out for possible pickpockets, and Jacques could only pay with cash. The unloading completed, Jacques' van and my small car were still at customs.

We then rented two trucks to transport our belongings to my uncle's house. Throughout the journey, we had to keep an eye out to prevent the drivers from taking another route and us from being scammed. When we returned to my uncle's house, he and his wife saw three heavily loaded vehicles. They were speechless. From the reality of their faces, I could read: "Where are you going to put all this?" In reality, I too had made the same thought. I was ashamed. Every time I tried to talk to Jacques about it, he raised his hand while shouting at me: "I don't need to hear what you're going to say, shut up and shut your mouth."

All my advice was deemed inadmissible. Tired of war, I let him do it from now on. For their part, my uncle and his wife have managed to classify all our belongings.

They were everywhere: on the upper and lower galleries in the drawing-room, in our bedroom, and in the courtyard, etc. Not to mention the belongings that had been stolen during customs clearance and transport. I felt embarrassed that I had caused so much trouble to so many people.

Jacques, on the other hand, did not care at all to disturb the private lives of others. I suggested that he rent a warehouse. "Too many thieves!" he objected. It wasn't wrong, but it was obvious that we couldn't stay any longer at my uncle's house. I reminded him that it was he who had insisted on this trip to Haiti and that, to satisfy him, I had given him all the money I had. So it's now up to him to manage to settle us properly somewhere.

We lacked the money to clear our vehicles through customs. Jacques recognized that we had to find a solution. I told my uncle about it. He agreed to let us use one of the entrances to his two parking lots to place objects for sale. The next day, we started our impromptu business. Believe it or not, buyers immediately showed up. In two days, we raised enough money to clear the van through customs, but there was still the small car.

Jacques thought that we could get it back later. Intended to keep some money for personal expenses. He had also decided to convert the van into a taxi. I disagreed, but my objection mattered little to him.

Life in Haiti was becoming unpleasant. This constant heat continued to bother me, and I couldn't get used to the mentality of my pregnant fellow citizens. I felt like I was on another planet. Jacques, on the other hand, was very fond of strangers, as well as of servants and court boys. He seemed very happy in Haiti. At one point, he swore to me that nothing in the world would make him return to Montreal.

Despite his attitude of indifference towards me, in the evenings, he demanded that I have sex with him. He alleged that he was back in his country, a hot country where you can do what you want, and that I had to satisfy his sexual desires at all times. And he continued: "My daughter, get ready, come and give me my vitamin."

I suffered immensely from his behavior. I then realized that by accompanying him to Haiti, I had ingenuously let myself be caught in his trap.

From the first day of my return to Haiti, I had the strong impression that I had chosen the wrong country. I hadn't been back since 1987, so it had been 10 years. Of course, many things had changed.

Present moment

Tuesday, November 14, 2006

5:15 p.m. Since Friday afternoon, I have made a stop. I couldn't go on writing. I was preoccupied with other things and I was a little unwell. Natatsha's children, Elle-Camy and Mikaël, you had the day off and you came to spend two days at my house, on Friday and Saturday. I was very pleased with your presence; At least I felt less alone. On Saturday night, my sister and I went to dinner at our friend Madeline's.

That evening, I was not well; That's why I came back around midnight. My sister had invited me to sleep at her house; Despite my tiredness, I preferred to go and sleep at home in my cozy bed with my six soft pillows.

On Sunday, I spent the day at home in my pajamas. I meditated and thought about my situation. I took care of myself, my mind. I needed it.

I continue my story.

Jacques didn't want to help me reintegrate into the country. At first, things were going pretty well before our luggage arrived in Haiti. But after customs clearance, everything changed. I went to Miragoâne, my hometown. When I got in, I was shocked to the point that I had a fever during the night. The city was dirty. An almost indescribable smell emanated from it. The city of Miragoâne that I had written in the first volume of my book had a complement changed to become a real dump. Allow me to present the new portrait, as faithful and objective as possible

Miragoâne from the 1990s to the present day

As I pointed out in the first volume of the book, Miragoâne is one of the five districts of the Grande-Anse department south of Port-au-Prince.

The architecture of the city has not changed since my first description. But the friendly and warm atmosphere, the peaceful atmosphere, and the impeccable maintenance of the place no longer reign there. However, its economy has grown greatly. With these large boats docking at the port, filled with goods, the municipal authorities could make an effort to repair the roads and restore the city's health. This one is like a real dump.

Part Two
Thursday, November 16, 2006
Present moment

7 a.m. You will excuse me, my dear children, because these days I cannot concentrate. Ideas get confused in my head. These are events that I wanted to erase from my memory. Then, in my effort to find them, I experience agonizing difficulties, and I suffer from them. I ask my angel to guide me and give me the inspiration I need. I'm going to try to do meditation and Tai Chi; I will certainly benefit from it.

The first steps in Haiti

When we arrived in Haiti, we went to live with my uncle because he was the only one who agreed to receive us. All the other members of the family were opposed to me going back to live in this country, especially with Jacques. After only a few days spent with him. I found that they were absolutely right.

After a few days in Haiti, I went to see them all. There was my niece Yolaine, who is a doctor, who lived in Tabarre (the Plain) in a large house with her husband Dane, her son Samy, and her younger sister Karola. And my niece, who is an agronomist and who also lives, also in La Plaine with her husband. My sister Claire lived 100 kilometers from the capital, in Miragoâne, with her husband, Goslin.

I immediately renewed my family ties with them. Jacques had family too, but. He did not solicit any services from her. I was the pillar and the foil; the one he always put forward when the time came to make major decisions.

He was always in the background to tell me what to do and whom to ask for a particular service. He had recourse to me only to satisfy his ambitions, his desires, his needs for money and for sex;

that was all. He had a way of doing things that made me feel compelled to give in to him. He was very cunning. He used me like a puppet!

We went to buy the license plates for the van. The process lasted two days. We ended up getting them by paying a bribe to a civil servant.

In the meantime, Jacques has begun to reassemble his trailer, which he had brought in parts from Montreal; he intended to use it to transport some belongings to my niece Yolaine in Tabarre. At Jacques's insistence, I had previously asked her husband for a little space in their property to store some of our luggage. They made available to us the largest room in the house, which was supposed to serve as their living room, but which was empty at the time.

It took Jacques seven hours to reassemble the trailer, with the help of my uncle's court boy. As soon as we arrived in Haiti, he took on as an auxiliary. Towards the end of the day, Jacques set out to transport some belongings there, first the furniture, appliances, materials, equipment, etc. The next day, he was done. There were still a few accessories left at my uncle's, but they were actually less cumbersome. And since we were still staying at my uncle's house, I felt a little relieved and much less embarrassed.

Present moment

Many thoughts were stuck in my memory. They are fully mixed up and want to go out at the same time. All this annoys me. I also have too many things to do at the same time. I feel overwhelmed.

I continue my story

Jacques, whom we remember, had decided to transform the van into a taxi. To do this, he had to modify the rear of the truck by erecting a roof and installing two rows of benches. In order to have a comfortable space during work, we went to my niece's house in La Plaine. The backyard of his property was very large and very peaceful. Jacques could therefore work on it in complete tranquility. Dionysius, the court boy, accompanied him.

While they were busy at their work, I watched them sit on the gallery. Or I would indulge in a little reading. I also took the time to admire nature, my niece's property leading me to forget the distant inconveniences of the Haitian capital. I have the serenity and the climate of peace that it offered.

The transformation of the van took two days. On April 9, 1996, Jacques began working on the road to Port-au-Prince. I had opposed him attempting this adventure, but once again, his reaction was very harsh: "That's enough! Here, I'm in charge! For passenger transport, there are two passengers: the driver and an assistant, the latter is called by the nickname 'secretary". He is stationed at the back of the vehicle to keep an eye on the passengers and make sure they pay their dues. It was Dionysius, the court boy, who acted as secretary.

They left in the morning at 4 a.m. to return at noon and leave at 3:30 p.m., to return around 7 p.m. On Saturdays and Sundays, they did not work. We would then go to Miragoâne or Les Cays, Jacques' hometown, where his cousin, a dentist, lived. We had visited him as soon as we arrived in Haiti and we had slept at his house. He had welcomed us very well, so much so that he had advised Jacques: "Why don't you come and live in Les Cayes? You and your wife will be more comfortable there. ». Jacques had declined the offer.

Some days, as I was unoccupied during the afternoon, I accompanied Jacques. I had the opportunity to visit different districts of the capital. Sometimes, he dropped me off at the home of a friend, Joséphine, in Pétionville, director of a small pre-kindergarten.

On the road to Pétionville, I liked to watch the painters and sculptors at work, and I admired their works. From the top of

Pétionville, I had a breathtaking view of a large part of the capital and I dominated the hills where rich citizens had built real castles.

Throughout the month of April, a routine had set in: the coming and going of work, the tours in Miragoâne at the end of the week. At the same time, Jacques picked up passengers in the back of the van to drop them off in Miragoâne. He never tired of repeating: "I don't do anything for nothing here, and everything I do is to raise money." He was happy with the turn of events, especially since I don't think he has any problems. I let him do what he wanted, and I gave him what he wanted when he ordered it.

Usually, when we go to Miragoâne, we sleep at my friend Nélia's house. She and her husband, Simon, had spent nearly 17 years in Montreal. They had returned to live in Haiti, but their four children had remained in Montreal. They owned a fairly spacious house on Bel-Air Street, very close to the cemetery. During the day, I went to my sister Claire's to observe the merchants; I also had pleasant conversations with my brother-in-law, Gostin.

On Easter weekend, Good Friday, my uncle and his wife invited us to a pilgrimage to the hill in Port-au-Prince, the Calvary of Miracles.

After a few weeks, I no longer wanted to stay with my uncle. It was too hot, and no electricity. At night, I could hardly fall asleep. The successive nightmares, the noise of cars and trucks, the noise of neighbors, the mosquitoes, I couldn't take it anymore. One night, I suddenly woke up from a dream where I saw a large snake lying on top of me in bed. I was always scared at night; it was too dark.

I was getting more and more nervous, but I was doing everything I could to make sure that no one, including Jacques, would notice. We had no financial problems, but I found the prospect of continuing to stay with our hosts unbearable.

I told Jacques that we were renting a house, but he turned a deaf ear. When I pointed out to him that the couple, especially my uncle's wife, wanted us to leave, he objected that I was making up stories.

I told my niece Yolaine and her husband about it. I told them of my dismay. They offered me to come and live with them with Jacques. We will pay the maid for our washing and other small services. This news delighted Jacques. He seemed so thrilled that I felt like he was expecting it and had already made his plan.

We informed my uncle of our plan to move to Yolaine's house. He expressed his agreement to us. I was very happy to leave. Afterwards, we went to visit them every time we went to Miragaône or Les Cayes. At the same time, we brought them provisions.

This was the first step in our experience in Haiti.

Part Three

The second stage of our experience in Haiti
At my niece Yolaine's house

In Haiti, I found the time unpleasantly long, the days never ended, even though I had only been in the country for two months. It was like I had been living there for over a year.

We arrived in the middle of March; and we left my uncle's house at the end of April. Since we had already transported the bulk of our rings to my niece's house, the little that was still at my uncle's house would be easier to move; it was actually done in one day.

I will now describe my niece's property and its environment. This situation will be fully justified by the course of events.

My niece's house is located in Tabarre, 15 minutes from the airport, inside the main road of the international airport. To get there, you have to take a small road that is very bumpy, which becomes very muddy when it rains. Since it is very narrow, one should drive slowly to avoid damaging the cars. Jeeps and vans are probably better suited to this type of road. We know that most of Haiti's small roads are in poor condition. Those who drive have become accustomed to it and are taking it carefully.

The property is bounded by a block fence with a large metal gate. Inside the courtyard are two large houses. The first belongs to my niece Yolaine and her husband Dane, and the second to Dane's brother.

These houses are surrounded by a garden and flowering shrubs. In the courtyard, the small house of the servant, that of the court boy, the traditional kitchen, and the latrines. Further on, at the bottom of the garden, an artesian then

My niece's house had a large porch in front and one in the back. I liked to get up early in the morning and sit on one of the galleries to pray, read, and write. I was impregnated by the calm and the smell of the morning dew. It was my favorite time of the day.

There were three exit doors: one at the front, one at the back, and one on the right side that looked out onto the garden.

In the entrance was a small living room. Adjacent to the dining room. Two large bedrooms are separated by one from the hallway, between the living room and the kitchen. One was the master bedroom, and the other was that of the son, Samy, and Karola was Yolaine's niece. Next to the living room was a large room, which must have been the large living room. As it was not fitted. We made it available to us. We put away in this room some of our personal belongings, as well as Jacques' tools, and the rest, we put everything that was left in the yard warehouse.

That night, I was able to sleep comfortably in my bed after unpacking a few boxes and placing my clothes in my desk drawers. I was also able to run the fan for part of the night, since in Tabarre, the electric current was supplied for a longer time. (This was the neighborhood of the private residence, President Aristide.)

As soon as I ventured outside, towards the end of the afternoon, I became the target and prey of mosquitoes. In particular, a critter locally called "bigaille". I tried to run away from her, but without much success. The effects of his sting manifested themselves in a small sore, perhaps an allergic reaction. My blood seemed to magnetize mosquitoes, while I had an aversion to them. I also hated the "anolis". These would come in unexpectedly and could jump on someone. They inspired me with morbid fear.

I have already noted that I dread the opaque black of Haitian nights. Jacques, however, very often invited me to go for a walk to buy griot (made with pork) and "fried sweet potatoes". I was apprehensive about the small road without electricity. During the journey, I would furtively close my eyes, and when Jacques spoke to me, I didn't answer. Since my arrival in Haiti, I was constantly told horror stories, which inspired me with feelings of constant insecurity. Jacque, on the contrary, seemed to have nothing, absolutely, nothing.

From the day we came to live with my niece, my relationship with Jacques improved. He continued to work during the week. I hardly went to Miragoâne on weekends anymore. At first, we went to Mass on Sundays with my niece and her husband. Then I put an end to it, since I was the only one who continued to go there. I must point out that the church was perched on a hill and that I considered it dangerous to make the journey without a trusted person by my side. Finally, I said my prayers, while sitting on the porch.

Even though things were going well with Jacques now, I missed my children and my family in Montreal very much. Especially Natatsha's little baby. She-Camay, who was only two months old when I left Montreal. I felt guilty. I imagined that they needed me. Especially since Mother's Day was approaching; In Haitian custom, it was the last Sunday in May. I had then received a card and a small gift from my daughter, which had moved me a lot. My son had also sent me a card. I called them sometimes, but not often, because the telephone service office was far from home. I could only get there by car, which was not the easiest because of the traffic jams.

My niece had invited us to a conference and graduation ceremony for the students of the laboratory at the Holiday Inn hotel in Port-au-Prince. I had prepared everything for the ceremony that was to take place on a Sunday during the month of May. I think it was Mother's Day Sunday. The night before, Jacques told me that he would not go. I tried to reason with him by pointing out that since our return to Haiti, we were not going anywhere and that it would be good for us to meet other people, which would facilitate our reintegration into the country. He told me that he was already integrated and that I was the one wasting my time on nonsense. "Even if you don't go, I'm going with Yolaine!" I told her. It remained ice-cold.

So I went with my niece and her husband to the conference. Before I left, Jacques asked me to leave him some money, because he would need it. Which I did.

Did you say, I didn't regret going to this ceremony at all. We arrived very early, an hour early, especially because my niece was the headmistress of the school. I hadn't had time for lunch. I then told my niece that I would take the opportunity to go to the hotel restaurant for lunch. When I got there, I spotted a table that contained everything we wanted for lunch. A waiter immediately assigned me a seat. After taking my order, he invited me to go and choose other dishes.

I had a very good lunch, and I felt happy with my gesture. It had been a long time since I had enjoyed such a good lunch since my return to Haiti. I then thought of my children, while saying to myself: "Today is Mother's Day in Montreal, Jacques didn't even wish me a happy Mother's Day. At least I enjoyed myself. I was proud of myself. I was not at all worried about the reaction that Jacques would show. It was my precious little moment of happiness.

When we came back, Jacques was absent. As soon as he reappeared, he started to play the indifferent. I acted as if I didn't realize it, and, in any case, his attitude didn't make me cold or hot, but above all, I wanted to extend my small happiness by a day.

The next day, Jacques changed his mood. He became excessively aggressive. Now, according to him, he was no longer interested in staying in Port-au-Prince. He was looking for the little beast, and he kept telling me that we should go and live in Les Cayes. Becoming aggressive too, I still accepted the idea of going to stay in Les Cayes for two or three weeks soon, on a trial basis. And then, we'll see, He welcomed my proposal.

In the meantime, my brother **Alain, who lived in New York, came to live with his wife** in Haiti. They already owned their house in the Delmas 31 district. Their rehabilitation in the country was looking good.

Mother's Day is celebrated in Haiti on the last Sunday of May. My niece and her husband invited us for the occasion to accompany them to a friend's house for the occasion. I was very willing to accept their offer, but Jacques was not. So, I felt obliged to stay at home with him to avoid complications. That day, as for Mother's Day in Montreal, he didn't say happy Mother's Day, no card, nothing at all. Instead, I was insulted because I had revealed to my niece that he was the one who had refused to let us go out with them. In short, I had a very bad time. I can't take it anymore. I've been crying for the whole day.

One evening, Jacques took me to the teleco to call the children in Montreal. He dropped me off at a company office located not far from Delmas Street at 7 p.m. I waited for him, waiting for him until 10 p.m. The teleco had then closed its doors, and it was dark; there was no longer a cat around. Just a few vans that were always full of passengers and didn't serve the area where I lived, anyway.

Fear was rising in me. Noticing a taxi, I signaled it to stop. Before taking my seat, I prayed to Jesus to protect me. My heart was pounding. I gave my address to the driver. I tried to talk to the driver in the manner of a typical Haitian woman in the country to avoid betraying my condition as a "diaspora" (returning from abroad). I kept quiet. I had given my uncle's address, at the rue Lumumba, near Delmas 9

When I arrived at my destination, I told the driver. As it was dark, I had prepared my money before getting into the taxi. When I gave him the amount of the ride, he kindly confessed: "Madam, why are you afraid of me? From the way you speak, I know you're a foreigner." Do not be afraid, I will do you no harm. go and knock at the barrier; I am waiting here, because it is too dark for you to remain alone in the street. He added, "Next time, don't stay away like that late. Fortunately, you have found me, because there are not many like me. Having thanked him effusively, I went to knock at the barrier. People were already in bed, because it was 11 p.m. They were even scared. The court boy, Denys, let 10 minutes pass before coming to open the door. My uncle went downstairs to check who had come knocking on his house at that late hour.

After expressing his feverish concern, he asked me what I was doing outside at such a late point in the night. I explained to him what had happened, namely that Jacques had never come back to get me. He and his wife were very angry about this; at the same time, they feared that something serious had happened to Jacques. Half an hour later, Jacques showed up at my uncle's house. He knocked on the barrier. He did not seem to be worried about everything. "I'm coming to get Enice," he said. My uncle told him he was unhappy, to which he did not react. He just said, "I knew she would come here." My uncle replied, "She might have died too." Jacques simply smiled and then addressed me with these words: "Come, let's go home."

My niece and her husband were also extremely worried. They thought we had been attacked. No one at home had gone to bed yet. I explained the events to them. In turn, they expressed their anger at Jacques, who once again did not connect. My niece had always strongly recommended that she not drive late at night. He laughed at it and maintained that nothing untoward could happen to him. He let people believe that they feared him to the highest degree.

I forgot to mention that as soon as I got into the van, he started calling me all kinds of names. He swore to me that he didn't need a woman like me who can't manage to get by, for example, to sit in the back of a public transport vehicle, etc. He felt that he did not have time to take care of a woman-child in Haiti. That I would never be able to live up to a hard-working, determined, manual-skilled person, like most women in the country.

From that day on, I began to quietly concoct a plan to get out of the Haitian bee-eater. I knew that Jacques was very clever and that I would have to maneuver subtly, while pretending to agree with everything he said or did. I was learning to be as clever as he was hypocritical with me, without him realizing it.

Sunday, November 19, 2006

11 a.m. Hello little ones, I'm back this morning a little tired. Last night, I stopped writing because I had to go babysit Analicia and Isaiah for three hours. When I arrived, Yole put them to bed, and they were happy to see me. They wanted to stay with me in the living room. I told them that they had to go to sleep. I sang the song to them, "My little Jesus, good evening." This made them sleep.

To relax, while waiting for Yole to return, I watched a movie. When I got home, it was 1 a.m. I had trouble falling asleep. When I was finally able to do so, I had terrible nightmares all night long. At 5 a.m., the phone rang, I woke up with a start. When I answered, the person hung up. I went back to sleep. This time I was able to sleep in peace. I got up at 9 a.m. For me, it's a reasonable time because today is Sunday. I think I should continue writing the book. If I want to finish the project!

Part Four

The Sorry Cayenne Experience (1996)

Jacques had continued his reproaches and acts of malice against me. One day, he said to me: "I think we should go to Les Cayes as I suggested. You promised me that you would come for a week to see if you could live there. He let me know that if he was so nervous, it was because he didn't feel comfortable at my niece's house and didn't really like Port-au-Prince. I objected that we should rent a house in Miragoane instead. This choice would cost us less and we could then open a pharmacy, a bakery or a small shop. And I'd be able to work in one of the banks in town or help my friend Nélia at her little school. There were many other options available to us. We owned a plot of land in Chalon, which would allow us to build a house.

His reaction was prompt: "We're going to Les Cayes first, and then we'll see." He was then thinking of the house of his cousin, a dentist, whose apartment above was booked. Planned to rent it to him. But I couldn't see myself living in this place at all, far from my family. Especially since when I go to Les Cayes, I feel even further away from my children and mine. I prayed. I begged God to work a miracle on my behalf.

But as Jacques had decided, we left for a week in Les Cayes. It was a long road. When we arrived in Miragoâne, we called his cousin at his clinic to warn him of our imminent arrival.

It had been a long time since we had been to Les Cayes. The cousin did not know that Jacques had converted his van into a taxi. Personally, I had always opposed Jacques working as a taxi driver in Haiti. I kept telling him, "You can't have left Canada to come and do this job here. There are many other possible professions. Do something else. If not, it would be better to go back to Montreal. You already have a clientele, and it worked very well for you. He replied: "I will never go back to Montreal. I prefer to ask for charity. He added: "If I take a taxi, it's quick money, and I feel free." »

I, on the other hand, didn't feel good about myself in Haiti. And I asked myself a lot of questions. Jacques was of the opinion that if someone was not happy, it was his problem. Since we were in a free country, everyone could do as he pleased, and so much the worse for the others!

When we arrived, his cousin was on the balcony. Usually, when we were introduced, the court boy would come and open the garage door to let the van in. This time, he didn't move. We went up with our luggage. His cousin's wife welcomed us well. She had our belongings deposited in the guest room, a large room with a very comfortable toilet. Then we went to the balcony to greet the cousin.

He immediately asked Jacques why he had modified the van. My husband told her that it was to ride a taxi, to transport customers. Cousin: "Do you take a taxi in Port-au-Prince?" And Jacques replies proudly: "Yes!" The other did not say a word to him. He went out. I was ashamed of Jacques; the moment was very humiliating, but it didn't seem to bother him.

At supper, the atmosphere was very cold, with almost no conversation. With me, the wife was very nice, as was her husband. But, given the situation, I didn't talk much. The next day, Jacques left to work on the road to Les Cayes by doing the Cayes-Cavaillon route, a distance of about 80 kilometers. He came back at the end of the day with very little money earned. For my part, during the day, I accompanied the lady to her shop, which was on the second main rue des Cayes. At least I could distract myself by watching the passers-by and the people shopping. I tried to make Jacques understand that it would not be possible to stay a whole week in

Les Cayes. This was not at all his opinion, for he was tempted in this city. As far as I was concerned, on the contrary, there was no question of renting an apartment there. I pointed out to him that his cousin obviously did not like his occupation as a taxi driver. Then I told him that I wanted to return to Port-au-Prince immediately. My outing did not delight him at all.

My diary
June 14, 1996

I haven't written for some time. Yet I have a lot to say. So much so that I don't know where to start.

I came with it to Les Cayes to spend a week. Everything was fine. Until I started talking to him about our stay and our plan to live here. I told him that I would not come to live here. In the evening, there was a radio program on divorce cases. He asked me if it concerned us. I told him that it would be disrespect, humiliation, malice, and hypocrisy that would cause our separation.

He then started to say stupid things to me, totally unreasonable things. Of things that hurt me. He even shouted at me, "If a man can't sleep with his wife as he wants, it's normal for him to have a mistress, because the mistress agrees to satisfy all his desires." He has said many other hurtful things to me.

I continue my story.

In the end, we didn't stay all week at Jacques' cousin's house. On the return trip, in the van, he put on very loud music so that he didn't have to talk to me. I had told him that I wanted to go through Miragoâne. Arriving in Desruissaux, we entered Miragoâne before continuing our journey to Port-au-Prince. We stayed there for just an hour. I told my friend Nélia and my sister Claire that I would come to spend the feast of St. John the Baptist with them in Miragoâne After that, we returned to Port-au-Prince.

Monsieur was not at all happy with my decision about Les Cayes. Our relatives in the capital were surprised to see us return so quickly. Without Jacques' knowledge, I told everything to my niece and her husband; They agreed with me. I confided to them that I would try to convince Jacques to accompany me to Miragoâne, for the feast of St. John, and at the same time; we would inquire at the same time about houses for rent. I returned to Port-au-Prince on June 15. From that date, until we left for Miragoâne, Jaques made me live hell once again.

My diary, June 22, 1996

I don't think I'm ready to write everything that shakes up my head yet. I need to find peace to do it.

It is 6:30 a.m. The weather is nice; I'm sitting on the porch at Yolaine and Dany's. Every morning, I get up at 6 a.m. to sit outside, not to watch the passers-by, given the height of the fence. But, to admire nature, the beautiful blue sky, the dew on the leaves, and the flowers.

While having my coffee, I look at Yolaine's two dogs, who do not stop playing with the goats. Then I do my morning prayer and do a little stretching. I feel alive, I can read within myself, and I meditate. In those moments, I feel like I am in control of myself.

If I don't do it one morning, I feel like my day isn't complete. These little moments of happiness belong to me. I don't share them with anyone, because I like to live in peace.

Our stay in Miragoâne, June 1996
The feast of Saint-Jean-Baptiste

For this part of my stay in Miragoane, I had written it in my diary. I transcribed it almost as it was.

July 3, 1996

I went to Miragoâne on Sunday, June 23, 1996, on the eve of Saint-Jean-Baptiste Day. The next day, I went to church. I filmed the mass. It was really beautiful. Residents of Miragoane had cleaned up the town and beautified the church in preparation for the celebration.

I met people I hadn't seen in years. For this occasion, everyone was well dressed. There had been a ball. I hadn't been there. After Mass, the whole family gathered at my sister's house for dinner, and the family from Port-au-Prince was also present.

My brother Alain, his wife Ida and my uncle Giordani, and I went to visit other families and friends, among them Vivianne's sister. It was very good; I had a great day.

I had planned to stay a week in Miragoâne. On the evening of the 24th, I went to sleep at my friend Nélia's house, who lives on Bellaire Street. Jacques wanted to return to Port-au-Prince the same evening or the next day. I let him know that I wasn't leaving right away. I was planning to stay for a week. He got all over the place. The next morning, he put my belongings back in the van, shouting that I was going back with him to Port-au-Prince.

When I got into the van, he told me that he wasn't going to Port-au-Prince, but to Les Cayes. I asked him to take my sister Claire's house in Bord-de-Mer Street and leave me in peace. He was therefore obliged to leave me at Miragoâne. I realized that I was enraged. He dropped me off at Claire's, where I spent the week with Fabienne and Nélia.

I spent a good week without him. For once, I had peace. He didn't stay in Les Cayes. The next day, Tuesday, on leaving Les Cayes, he stopped at Miragoâne to inform me that he was returning to Port-au-Prince. I wished him good luck by reiterating that I was staying in Miragoâne. It was a truly wonderful week. I attended to my sister at her store. Occasionally, I would cross across Fabienne's house to joke with her. I used to walk in the streets in the evening on my way to my friend's house on Bellaire Street. It was the graduation ceremony of his students. I helped her prepare for the party.

The graduation party took place on Sunday, June 30. Jacques came back to pick me up on Monday, July 1st.

I was proud to realize that for once, I had been able to stand up to Jacques.

Part Five

Preparing for my return to Montreal

I don't know what happened then. I find Jacques very calm. However, in such circumstances, it is because he is certainly preparing a bad move. Before I left Miragoâne, Max had called me to tell me that he would send a plane ticket for me alone so that I could come and attend the baptism of my granddaughter Elle-Camay, my daughter's child.

Jacques was completely opposed to this plan to travel to Montreal, while I felt the need to see my children again and to see a doctor. The day after our return from Miragoâne, on Tuesday, July 2, 1996, Jacques warned me to tell him immediately if I was seriously planning to go to Montreal.

He warned me that until he had my answer, he would do nothing; He would lie in bed until I revealed my real intentions to him. He wasn't kidding. I sensed something suspicious was brewing under his unusual good humor. He was finally about to move on to the execution of his project.

It was 9 a.m. After undressing, he went to bed. At about 4 p.m., I wrote him a letter in which I reiterated my firm resolution to go to Montreal, followed by my reasons.

After reading the letter, he got up from bed and said, "Now you can consider us separated." When he works, he keeps no money on him because of thieves; it is always to me that he entrusts the recipe. That day, he took all the money back. He didn't leave me a cent. He then told me, "I'm the one who will keep the money from now on, and you'll tell me how you're going to go about going to Montreal now." He continued, "I now forbid you to ask me questions about my activities." I didn't say a word

When I think about that, it is thanks to me and my money that Jacques returned to Haiti! I had made considerable sacrifices for the realization of this trip. I had released my retirement funds, sold my jewelry. And I had agreed to part with those who were weary to me, dearest to me in this life: my children and my two-month-old daughter, in addition, I had also had to distance myself from my sister who is furious with me because of Jacques.

In the evening, despite this mortifying day, the man still wanted to make love to me anyway. It's really disgusting. It was truly revolting. He did it by making threats and with gestures of rage. If I had been able to leave before the scheduled date, I certainly would have done so, because I felt absolutely depreciated and totally demoralized, I didn't want to stay in Haiti anymore. I had to empty the place as quickly as possible. I still had a week left, which I found inordinately long.

July 5, 1996

Today is my daughter Natatsha's birthday. I went to the Teleco to call him, to wish him a happy birthday. The lines were not working. I went to wait for Jacques at my brother Alain's. He came to pick me up around 4:30 p.m. He had his cunning air. He wanted to find my passport. He looks for it everywhere. I know him well enough to know that I should hide my passport. He looked for it everywhere. Knowing it very well, I knew I had to hide this one. He would not find it. He had this way of asking me questions to lure me into a trap. I had to be constantly on my guard not to be caught.

Before July 5th, I hadn't written anything because it was a week of hell that I had lived through with Jacques. Rapes, acts of pure malice, bad deeds. What was more serious, since we were staying with my family, I couldn't shout in my defense. One day, I briefly talked about it with Dane, my niece's husband. "There's nothing we can do about it," he said. He's your husband. If we intervene, he may become even more brutal with you. Be patient, because very soon you will be leaving for Canada. I have tried to arm myself with patience, but when one suffers, one becomes fatally impatient. Especially since my trip was delayed by a few days, because there was no room left on the date I wanted to travel.

July 8, 1996

It is now that I realize how crazy I was to come to Haiti with Jacques. During our time here, he sought to humiliate me more and more every day. I had my lesson. There's nothing in the world that's going to make me reconsider my decision, except God, because you never know. But one thing is for sure: I suffered terribly.

July 9, 1996

When Natatsha had her baby, she had suffered a lot. I had to bring her to my house for a month with the baby and Patrick because he had just been operated on, too. This situation had imposed a lot of work on me, but I had fulfilled it with joy.

Very exhausted at that time, I got caught up in Jacques' games. I woke up in Haiti after two months. I made an atrocious mistake in going back with Jacques. On the other hand, I went all the way. Experience. Now I can say that I know the man perfectly. If I had listened to my family and Aunt Dadia when I made this brief stay in New York... But let's move on! It's too late, I'm going to get out of it, but deprived entirely of resources! I'm going to leave everything; I want to save my skin and my dignity. It's more important than anything else.

July 15, 1996

I was supposed to leave today, July 15, 1996, for Montreal. Unfortunately, Natatsha could not find an available flight until August 5. July 13 was our wedding anniversary. I didn't mention anything to Jacques. I still had a great evening, while the whole family was gathered at my brother Alain's house for another birthday. I had a lot of fun, and it felt good.

July 16, 1996

Today, I have to write, but it's really painful that I have on my heart, and it hurts a lot.

For the past week, Jacques has been forcing me to sleep with him every night for hours, and he starts it very brutally. He presses his hand over my mouth so that I don't scream. He squeezes me everywhere. He warns me that he will continue to attack it violently every night and sometimes even every day if there is no one else at home. He gave me this ferocious warning: I do what I want with you, with your heart, your vagina, and everything! "I have this right because you are my wife." He constantly addressed me with threats. I think he's mentally ill. I cried all the time. I can't wait to leave. He shouldn't do this to me, because I don't have any love for him anymore. And I don't belong to him.

In our sexual intercourse, I do not feel any pleasant sensation. So, I resigned myself and let her do what he wants

He seized all my cards: social insurance, health insurance, as well as all the important documents I had placed in my office. Fortunately, he couldn't find my passport. When I asked him if he had taken my IDs, he claimed that he had not taken anything. But I know him. He is exceedingly cunning.

July 22, 1996 — Journal

I opened my newspaper this morning. I couldn't write because my head is too full. That will be for another time. Maybe I'll be fine when I'm back in Montreal.

I am now forced to sell some personal belongings to be able to have the money I need for my trip. I have already pointed out that Jacques had recovered all the money. Luckily, I have a generous family who can help me.

I thank God for everything He has done for me. I sold my secretary and my chair to my niece Yolaine, which is a gesture of last resort for me since these objects represented a very high value in my eyes. At least I know that they stay in the family.

Present moment
July 28, 1996

I am on an American Airlines plane to New York. I haven't written since July 22 because I was preparing for my departure today, July 28. I exchanged my ticket for a detour to New York, thanks to the money from the sale of some furniture. Jacques owed money to my uncle. I repaid it, paid for my plane ticket, and brought a certain amount with me to Montreal. I have finally left Haiti, and I am happy! Thank you, Jesus!

Even though I left Jacques and Haiti, I still have a little sadness, because I had family and friends in Haiti. But I couldn't stand Jacques' behavior anymore. Living with him makes me suffer too much. To live together under the same roof, there is constant bickering, acts of hostility. He's like a demon. However, I noticed that as soon as he realized that I had decided to leave, he became as gentle as a sheep. Maybe it's his way of making amends, I don't know. As far as he knows, I no longer had time to consider all this, and I no longer had confidence. I think we should live far apart, for a while at least, and the future will tell the rest. I realized that with children, it was the same. He cannot endure family life. He is a man who manages better on his own. I pray that God will keep him and help him, because he is, in the end, a walking patient.

Jacques had come to take me to the airport. Fortunately, I would never have done it alone. Everyone was aggressive. It was downright unbearable. Looking at Jacques, I sent him a message in my mind: "Jacques, you don't know how you hurt me. Just thinking about it makes my heart ache. It was the second time I thought I was leaving Jacques.

10 p.m. *I stop, I'm tired, my back and my head hurt. I will take Advil tablets.*

A look back

When I left Jacques in Haiti, I felt no remorse; On the contrary, I felt delivered. I was coming out of a hell I had never imagined. Before I left for Haiti, an inner voice had warned me of the danger. But I didn't want to listen to him. My family wanted to warn me. But noticing my attitude, she finally gave up. I was then as if hypnotized. I couldn't see anything, and I couldn't hear anything. I let myself be caught in Jacques's trap.

Present moment
Tuesday, 21 November 2006

7:30 a.m. I slept very well. Throughout the night, I felt rocked or not protecting an angel. He whispered soft words in my ear and whispered in my ear something I couldn't understand, but what relaxed me? It had appeared on the face of my unknown friend. I felt relaxed.

I really needed this moment of calm because after last night's heartbreaking writing, I was deeply touched in my heart and in my self-esteem. I was afraid to close my eyes so as not to plunge back into nightmares, not to relive what I had experienced before leaving Haiti.

I tried to read, without success. I felt nervous. I prayed. I told God that I was putting my mind and heart in His hands. Sleep took me to another dimension. I was at peace. And I thanked God.

Present moment
Tuesday, 21 November 2006

8:30 a.m. *I'm going to take a break from writing for at least three or four days, because I have to complete the outline of the book in order to be able to continue my writing project. I'll leave it to you. See you.*

Chapter 4

A solo return to Montreal.

Part One

Back with My Kids 1996

Returning to Montreal after 4 months spent in Haiti via New York. Aunt Dadia picked me up at the airport. She was happy to see me. When I arrived at her house, I was very exhausted. Even though she had prepared a good dinner for me, I hardly ate that night. I was too tired. I expressed to him my desire to go to bed at once; I would give him news from Haiti the next day. At his insistence, I agreed to sleep in his room.

That night, I slept well. I took advantage of my stay in New York to regain my senses. I spent 5 days chatting with my aunt and resting. On August 3rd, I returned to Montreal. When I arrived, I went to live with my daughter. She was then living in an apartment on Saint-Denis Street, at the corner of Beaubien. She lived with her husband Patrick and her little daughter Elle-Camy, who was 6 months old, and also with their big dog Sisley.

I felt good at home. The accommodation was on the second floor. There was a large bedroom, a large hallway, a large living room, a kitchen adjoining a dining room, and a large balcony at the back that Patrick had tastefully arranged. I liked to sit in that place to relax and pray.

Every Sunday, we would go to Beaver Lake to calm down, pray to the angels, and meditate. On the highest slopes, we sat on the grass and looked at the clouds. We were watching those who had the shape of a human face, or an angel, or whatever. And then we would go to St. Joseph's Oratory to finish our prayers by asking God and the angels to protect and guide us. I loved visiting these places, which gave me great peace.

I took care of my granddaughter, who was a very calm baby. The big dog Sisley kept us company. One day, I was alone with the baby in the house; he was sleeping in his crib, and I took the opportunity to take a nap. It was early afternoon. I lay down in my daughter's bed and immediately fell asleep. I was in a dream state. I felt something next to me. I turned around, and I saw Sisley sleeping quietly behind me.

I immediately got up and shouted: "Sisley, get up, get out of bed." He didn't move. I left him there. After a few minutes, he got out of bed on his own and went to the living room. The baby and I couldn't go back to sleep.

Sisley loved the child. When she walked or crawled, the dog would stand in front of her so that she wouldn't fall or hurt herself. He was a good dog.

My daughter took advantage of my stay at her home to eliminate the excess weight gained during her pregnancy. She went to the YMCA every day for her exercise. For my part, I encouraged him to persevere.

I was very happy to be with them. My son came to see me very often, and I also went to visit him. He was still living in a rented house in my sister Irene's house on Laval Street. She had put it up for sale. On October 26, 1996, we threw a party for his girlfriend Yole's birthday. During the evening, Max surprised his girlfriend. He got down on one knee and proposed to her. She was overjoyed. Everyone shared their happiness. My daughter and I accompanied my son to buy the wedding ring. He was radiant.

Three months later, they moved to live together in another apartment on Sherbrooke Street West.

In the meantime, I continued to enjoy the happiness of being with my family. I was happy, but one particular fact bothered me. Jacques called very often to ask me when I was going to return to Haiti. At first, I whispered to my daughter to pretend that I was absent. I was thinking about a strategy that would allow me to get rid of him. Let's not forget that I had left it at my niece's house. I had to find a way out of it very diplomatically, remembering that he kept more than one trick up his sleeve, not to mention that he is a cunning man.

My niece from Haiti, Yolaine, and her little boy, Samy, and Aunt Dadia came to spend a few days in Montreal. They had gone down to my sister Irene's house. I didn't go to her house often because I was obviously not welcome. When I went there occasionally, it was to visit my brother.

For my sister's birthday, my niece, my aunt, Vivianne, and my sister's friends planned to surprise her. When I arrived, Irene was not there, and I quickly realized that I was not welcome at the party. They told me about the things that hurt me, and I wanted to take advantage of this day to recover my sister's friendship. I don't use the word "affection" because that was too much to ask. Just a little bit of friendship. I was kind of kicked out. I went out to get a taxi, my eyes all in tears and my heart heavy.

When I got into the taxi, I gave my destination address to the driver. He recognized me immediately. He exclaimed, "Mrs. Jacques, I didn't know you were back in Montreal!" He was a friend of Jacques. I just replied: "Ah! Yes, I'm here in Montreal. I couldn't say more, because I didn't want him to see my distress. At the same time, I wanted to avoid crying.

When I arrived at my daughter's house, I immediately burst into tears. I told him what had happened. She told me not to go there anymore and wait for everything to work out because every time I went to my sister's house, I came back unhappy. She concluded, "Take your time, mammy; we love you. We're going to help you get out of it, my brother, Patrick, and I.

Patrick, every time he saw me sad, told me stories to make me laugh. We would stay late in the living room chatting while the baby slept in the bedroom.

I had gotten into the habit of sleeping in the living room on a superfluous sofa. One evening, while I was sleeping, I felt that mosquitoes were biting me; I screamed for help. Almost immediately, I realized that I was dreaming. I had a lot of nightmares at that time, but I didn't worry too much. I wanted nothing in the world to disturb my moments of happiness with my little family. My daughter and I have, in the meantime, devised a strategy for me to return to Haiti to move Jacques from my niece's house. I prepared a list of elements of conduct during my stay in the country.

I left for Haiti on December 4, 1996, with money to rent the house and move. When I left Montreal, my project was methodically planned. I had planned two months to make everything. I was very optimistic. I felt morally strong. And at the same time, I was very suspicious. Because I had started to know the man I was dealing with well, or at least a little more.

In fact, I didn't know what was really waiting for me there. I mentioned earlier that Jacques called me very often to tell me to go back, but I was not well informed of his actions in Haiti, and he was not informed of my decisions either. We were both suspicious of each other.

Part Two
Another stay in Haiti

December 4, 1996
A second cover with Jacques.

When I arrived in Haiti, Jacques picked me up at the airport. I thought he was calm and nervous at the same time. He didn't talk much. He was in unkempt clothes. I was hot, and I found the country very desolate. I was on the verge of tears, but I didn't want Jacques to notice my sadness.

My niece's house was not far from the airport, and in less than 10 minutes we were at our destination. After taking the briefcases out of the van, since my niece and her husband had not yet returned from work, Jacques said to me, "I want to talk to you about what I did while you were away." To begin with, I operate a coal business. I buy coal in bulk on the road to Les Cayes. I store it in a warehouse that Dane rented me in his yard. The maid and the waiter find me customers. He said that the company was working very well. That it could bring in a lot in the short and long term. I told him that it was very good, that I was happy for him. "There's one more thing," he said, and then paused, while looking at me. I blurted out: "Speak, I'm listening!" He continued: "I have a dump truck that transports stones from La Boule to Port-au-Prince." I shouted, "Oh, yes?"

At first, I thought the truck belonged to him and that someone else was driving it. This was not the case. The vehicle belonged to a friend from Montreal who considered his driver very unreliable. Jacques had offered to take care of the truck and drive it himself until he could find a good driver. "Are you sure you can do this job?" I asked. He assured me that he did. I continued, "Jacques, aren't you going to tell me that you left Montreal to come and do the job of a dump truck driver? That's not possible! Especially since it's very dangerous to drive a big truck on the road to La Boule. »

He told me that I had no advice to give him. That he would act as he saw fit. "OK!" I said. I have added the form: nothing. But I said, "If that's what you like, that's fine." Good luck.

And we changed the conversation. I gave him some items I had brought him. I didn't tell him about my plan that night, because I realized that he was well involved in the neighborhood where he worked as well as in his business.

When my niece came back from work with her husband, Jacques was out. They took the opportunity to tell me about the truck and strongly suggested that I advise Jacques to return the truck to its owner. In fact, our two families and all our relatives agreed with this.

They said it was dangerous there, and especially that there was another driver before him driving the truck. You never know, he can do magic against Jacques. I let them know that I have already spoken to Jacques. And also, he was the one who did the mechanics of this big truck. He was very busy.

A few days later, I managed to talk to him about my project. Which I accomplished gently. I did my best to make it clear that my niece needed to take possession of her living room to complete the construction of the house. That we had better go to Miragoâne for two days to look for a house to rent. I stressed that I had the money. As it was a Thursday, I suggested that we come during the weekend; At least he would have time to come back on Sunday evening and return to work on Monday morning.

He accepted my plan to stay in Miragoâne. To my surprise, he seemed very receptive. In Miragoâne, we slept at my friend Nélia's house. I told him about the project. He had a book house next to her house, but I didn't like it, because it was too close to the cemetery. There was another house at the bottom of the town, near the crossroads at the main street before the new city.

Nélia was convinced that it would be a good place to run a business, especially a bakery, since the previous owner operated a bakery there. That would be ideal. The current owner was a former teacher with the Sisters of Wisdom. I knew her well, and Nélia was her friend. She sent her little protégé, Marjo, to warn her that we were planning to come and visit the house. It was then uninhabited.

The next day, we went to the scene. It was a large, very solid two-story brick house, with a balcony at the top and a gallery at the bottom, several rooms, a parking lot, and a courtyard. The toilet and kitchen are inside. It was a very good house.

As it was a Sunday, we were not able to meet the owner. We left and told our friend to inform the lady that we wanted to rent the house. Nélia had the cost of the rent. I suggested to Jaques that we come back during the indicated Christmas weekend to meet the landlady and sign the lease.

Thus, we would spend Christmas in Miragoâne, and then we would start the move. When I returned to Port-au-Prince, Jacques continued to work with the truck; A Day later, it broke down. Business was no longer going as well because Jacques didn't really know the job. Dionysius, his young secretary, was still working with him. He had no money left to pay it. He asked me to lend him a certain amount to buy repair parts and gasoline. He told me that the situation would improve, that he would pay me back soon and that I should not worry at all. I reminded him to be especially careful on a small mountainous road, because it was excessively dangerous.

Talking to him all week, I ended up with pain and misery convincing him to put the truck back. He resigned himself to it, because he realized that he was continuing to spend while the money "wasn't coming in."

One day, he invited me to come and see how tall and big the truck was. We were at my niece's house. When I got on it, I had the impression that people were very small because the truck was so huge. I panicked; my heart was pounding. "You're sick of driving a truck like that!" I reproached him. He replied that he was never afraid of anything.

On Friday, December 13, 1996, he went to work. The truck broke down. He was forced to leave the truck in a mine on the mountain. Someone dropped him and Dionysius off in Petionville. He called me to go and get them. When I arrived, he wasn't happy because he thought I had taken too long to do it.

I didn't reply, one of my friends, Christine, had invited me for the following Sunday to a bazaar and a mass at the Sisters of Wisdom's. I asked Jacques to join me. He accepted. But we didn't stay there long. He felt too tired. The day before, Saturday evening, he had asked me to accompany him the following Monday in the van, in order to pick up the truck that had broken down. He brought the part to repair it. He then planned to fill it with sand to go down the mountain. For my part, I would drive the van for the return.

That Monday morning, December 16, 1996, we left home very early. We went to pick up young Denys and went to the mine of La Boule. Jacques, after many attempts, ended up getting the truck to work. I may have forgotten to mention that Jacques was transporting sand from a mine quite far from the capital. Between him and his fellow truckers, there was fierce competition.

In the mine that day, the drivers behaved like rabid beings. The law of the jungle obviously applied to the scene. Everyone was screaming, including Jacques. He was mainly attacked. "Your diaspora," he yelled at. Leave! Return to the country from which you come!" In the meantime, an ineffable fright invaded me. As a powerless spectator of the scene, I sensed that at any moment a slippage could occur.

Noticing my growing anxiety, Jacques offered to drive me to the top of the hill and wait for him in the van, while he would take care of the loading of the truck. I nodded, even though I was afraid to stay there alone. From above, I watched those who did not stop insulting each other. There were many tipper machines, and also the tractors that loaded them. But the operation took time. Finally, Jacques' vehicle was loaded: He pulled it out of the bottom of the mine. I watched him come. The hand on the steering wheel and Denys at his side. He motioned for me to follow him. At this point, the road was made of crushed stone.

When we arrived on the high road, my feeling of fear did not dissipate; on the contrary. I couldn't drive anymore. I was sweating profusely, and my hands were cold. I honked my horn. Jacques sent his young assistant to take my place at the wheel of the van. Despite everything, I was still paralyzed by fear. We ended up leaving the main road to take the Boule road, which was a little safer. We tried to follow Jacques as carefully as possible. Désir shouted at me that Jacques was driving too fast on this steep hill. I didn't understand at the time. He repeated excitedly: "He's going too fast! We don't see him anymore! He's going to fall! I exclaimed, "Jesus, don't let him fall off the cliff!" We immediately saw a whirlwind of dust forming further ahead. It was Jacques' truck that had overturned at the foot of a cliff on the road to the boule.

Denys immediately started to accelerate, to such an extent that when we arrived at the scene of the accident, the van could hardly stop. The young man ended up stopping her just at the edge of the cliff. Very quickly, many curious people showed up. On learning from Dionysius that I was the wife of the injured man, one of them was moved: "Ah! The gentleman died instantly, and his wife almost went through it too. »

I will never forget the circumstances of this dramatic event. The young man went down like a madman to go and help Jacques. Fortunately, the truck did not actually fall on the side of the cliff, but on the side of the mountain.

It was totally buried under the load of sand. Dionysius, with his hands alone, managed to free the sand that buried Jacques. The latter had lost consciousness. Her lips all seemed purple. He was barely breathing. I brought it back, calling it reprise. Other men came to help Dionysius get him completely out of the sand. His left arm was badly bruised. He had a long-sleeved shirt whose fabric was very thick, and pieces of cloth and sand were mixed with his flesh. It was something distressing and painful to watch.

As I write this passage, I feel the same painful sensations that I had experienced at that moment. The condition of the arm caused me intense fear; it was flooded with blood. People helped as much as they could, but I felt that he did not take enough precautions. I asked them to let me hold the arm myself while they carried it. I held that bloody arm in my hands until the ambulance arrived, and at the same time, I kept talking to Jacques to keep him awake. The witnesses of the event showed sincere pity for us. And my heart ached. When the ambulance arrived, we put him there, and with Denys, I got into the van to follow them. At the Canapé vert hospital, Jacques was stretched out on a stretcher. I covered his arm with a sheet. He kept bleeding.

I then called my uncle, my brother, and my niece, who was a doctor, and she came right away. Hospital officials asked me if I had insurance. I told them that I was from Canada, but that I didn't have my cards with me.

My niece then went to the doctor in charge. They were colleagues. Almost instantly, we started taking care of Jacques. The doctor reported that the operation would require a blood transfusion. We had to go and buy some from the Red Cross. I went there with my niece Yolaine.

The Red Cross did not have Jacques' blood group, which was O-negative. We had a donor with this blood group type. He was skinny. My niece told me that she was going to advise the doctor to do his best not to transfuse this blood to Jacques, because she doubted its quality. I wasn't charged because my niece was a doctor. But I still gave the man some money.

The operation was carried out without delay. Jacques was very weak. Since he was diabetic, an endocrinologist was also called in. He was operated on during the night. And the operation was extremely long. At some point, I had lost track of time.

Present moment

Tuesday, November 28, 2006

Last night, I went to bed at one in the morning, but woke up with a start at 5:30 a.m. I dreamed that a friend of Jacques' came to pick him up for a new job. He asked me where his wine-red shirt was. He wanted me to go and get him from the cupboard myself. If she weren't there, I'd have to figure out how to find her.

In my dream, of course, I imagined living reality. I was sad and wondered when I would finally be able to get out of this mess. The shirt was from a terrible accident.

The friend who had come to pick up Jacques in the dream was wearing the same shirt with the dust on it. A strange dream, isn't it!

Part Three

The aftermath of Jacques' operation in Haiti

Jacques had been kept in the recovery room. I went to see him; he was still sleeping. It was daylight. I spent the rest of the night in the hospital waiting room. Although sofas were available, I couldn't sleep. I was intensely nervous and very worried. I thought I would need a lot of money as soon as possible. How prohibitively expensive it would be!

I was also thinking about the children in Montreal. I knew I had to call them. When he woke up, Jacques was taken to a private room. He did not talk much; The operated arm was in plaster with iron rods hanging outside.

After the operation, the surgeon came to talk to me. He tried to explain to me that he had done his best, that there was a lot of residue in the wound, that he had done temporary work, and that he would have to operate on it again. He had avoided a transfusion. I didn't understand what he was saying. Everything seemed unreal to me. He told me that the hospital administration would inform me of the costs of hospitalization and surgery. I hadn't slept all night. I washed myself and arranged a little in Jacques's room. I had a coffee to wake up, and around 9 a.m., I went to the administration office to meet the director. She explained to me how the hospital worked. One amount per day for the room, plus equipment expenses, bandages, gloves, cotton, alcohol, etc. Everything was separate. As far as doctors were concerned, they would determine the amounts of their fees themselves. There were four of them: the surgeon, the general practitioner, the endocrinologist, and the anesthesiologist.

The management demanded an initial amount to be able to keep Jacques in the hospital. And she said that in two days at most, I had to pay another amount.

I made the first payment with a few extra fees. I informed Jacques of my interview with the lady. And I pointed out to him that in order to raise all the money required for his hospitalization, I had to take certain steps as soon as possible. For example, calling the children, trying to take out a loan, selling personal property, etc. First of all, there was no question of selling his tools. In the end, he conceded, he had to be informed of the prices asked. I accepted his conditions. I then phoned Denys, Jacques's young assistant, who immediately came to pick me up at the hospital. I felt, of course, too nervous to drive myself. At my niece's request, her court boy would come in the meantime to keep Jacques company.

Once these arrangements were made, I called the children to inform them of the accident and ask them to send me as little as they could. My attempts to borrow were unsuccessful. I still had to sell a few tools, in preparation for the first payments to the doctor and the hospital. At the Canadian embassy I visited, an officer apologized for not being able to do anything to help me. In the meantime, I had completely forgotten about the possible recourse to the Société de l'assurance auto du Québec.

Jacques, for his part, flatly rejected the idea of returning to Montreal. While avoiding upsetting him about it, I thought, "After all, we'll see!" And I continued to struggle like crazy to take out a loan.

When I returned to my uncle's house, he gave me an amount that the children had sent me by transfer. Whew! What a relief. It was the day before, before I left the hospital, the doctor had warned me that if I didn't bring the second post the next day, he was still going to operate on Jacques to remove the iron rods from his wounds and close the arm in the cast. He was afraid that we would run away with his stems!

I had promised him that he would receive his money the next morning at 11 a.m. His words had proved to be extremely cruel. The reception of the transfer was timely

The day before, I had asked Jacques' sister, who lived in Port-au-Prince, to come and keep him company at the hospital, which allowed me to continue my loan efforts.

Unbeknownst to Jacques, I called the children and asked them to tell his doctor in Montreal that he had been in an accident and that, as soon as it was possible, I would go home with him to have him treated at Notre-Dame Hospital.

That evening, back at my niece's house, I informed the whole family that I intended to return to Miragoâne to sell part of our land in Chalon to pay our medical and hospital expenses and the doctors. My project was considered very reasonable.

The next morning, young Denys came to pick me up and drop me off at the hospital. We arrived there at 10 a.m. Jacques was absent from his room. His sister informed me that the doctor had come to pick him up very early to take him to the operating room to remove the metal rods. She had tried to assure him that I was coming to pay her money. In vain. He was convinced that we were planning to flee to Montreal with his equipment.

I was helpless. At the end of the operation, I pointed out to him that his behavior had been unprofessional. Clinically, he told me that at least he had managed to get his medical instruments back. His manner of acting had been truly shameful.

He insisted on getting paid on the spot. For my part, I asked him for a final, detailed invoice; I would pick up Jacques within two days and then pay the full medical bills.

When the doctor left, Jacques suddenly showed himself to be nervous. I had no choice but to tell him my plan to bring him back to Montreal on December 26, once the reimbursements related to his treatment had been made. I then had to tell him all the means mobilized for the projects (from my initiative) to raise the necessary amounts. I am leaving at this very moment for Miragoâne to sell part of the land. Your sister is here; she will take care of you.

A few minutes later, I was dropped off at the bus station to take the bus from Miragoâne. It was December 22. The journey from Port-au-Prince to Miragoâne took about two hours.

I first went to my friend Nélia's house. I told him everything that had happened and told him about my intentions. According to her and her husband, instead of selling my land, I would be better off resorting to a bank loan, offering the land as collateral. I accepted their suggestion. But as at the end of the day the bank was already closed, we went directly to the director of the company. My offer seemed to interest him keenly. When he learned, however, that a house not completely built occupied the land, he expressed his regret that he could no longer help me.

My friend and her husband then started a "word of mouth" advertisement relating to the extremely urgent sale of the land. My sister Claire and her husband immediately followed suit. It so happens that Claire, being a Protestant, began to inform the people of her church of my decision to sell the land.

In the early evening, I went up to Chalon to show potential buyers around the land. I fell twice while venturing into the woods. I almost broke my leg. I was exhausted and stressed to the maximum.

I stayed to sleep at Nélia's. After taking a shower, I tried to sleep, in vain, despite my extreme fatigue. The next day, December 23rd, my sister came to pick me up very early, around 5:30 a.m.

Along the way, she told me about two potential buyers and attestations of other land that were part of her father's inheritance. To his proposal to sell one of these locations. I replied that I would not do it for Jacques. I would only consent to sell the land belonging exclusively to him and me. I thanked him, but I will not sell our inheritance for Jacques.

We met the two interested persons and one of them, a notable of the city, accepted my prize, without reservation of approval from his son living in New York. In the early afternoon, he informed us that his son agreed, but that the transaction would not take place for another week. In the meantime, my brother-in-law Gostin was preparing a plan B negotiated with his rich cousin. I had an appointment with him for the next morning, December 24, 1997, at 11 a.m. In the meantime, the land would be surveyed in my presence, which was promptly done. In the evening, I went to sleep at my sister's house. At around 10:30 a.m. on December 24, my brother-in-law and I went to the home of the loaner cousin who owned a large two-storey house in the Grand-Rue de Miragoâne. He received us in his spacious dining room. After signing the papers of the field, I gave them away; For his part, he gave me a wad of cash. "No need to count them, he is reliable," my brother-in-law assured me.

The transaction concluded, we returned to my sister's house, where she was waiting for us in the company of her Protestant "sisters". She had prepared a delicious meal for me. These ladies welcomed me by singing praises of thanks to the Lord. Overflowing with joy, they all clapped their hands. "Eat, eat," my sister insisted, "you have to eat to keep all your energy!" And she was careful to add: "Glory to the Lord!" I applied his exhortation to the letter, foreseeing that I too needed extreme determination to face the challenges ahead.

After eating, I washed myself. As I had brought a large travel bag, which was almost empty, she placed the wads of cash at the bottom of the bag and covered them with a little laundry. Then she asked me if I was ready to leave. I said yes. She handed me the bag at the same time as her Christian friends sang a hymn. And she added these details: "No one is going to accompany you to the van that will take you to Desruisseaux. You are going alone, but the Lord will guide you throughout the journey and even after. Glory to the Lord; thank you, Jesus! I left without looking back.

The van that took me to the Desruisseaux intersection made the trip in a few minutes. I hurried into one of the few trucks that were going to Port-au-Prince on Christmas Eve. The candidates were jostling to take their seats. I managed to sit on a bag of coffee or rice, I don't know. Needless to say, we were packed like sardines. But suddenly I got scared and immediately got out of the truck.

Noticing an old school bus almost empty, I hurried into it, at the invitation of an assistant of the driver, I took the precaution of sitting very close to the door of the vehicle. About ten minutes later, it was crowded. While hugging the precious bag to my chest, I tried to move as little as possible while praying intensely. Most of the passengers were talking loudly and clearly. Some, impatient, harassed the driver, judging that he was not going fast enough; they insisted on meeting at home at all costs on Christmas Day. For my part, I feared an accident at any moment.

We finally arrived in Port-au-Prince at 6 p.m. I took a taxi to the Canapé Vert hospital. During the journey, fearing to betray my condition as a "diaspora", I tried to converse with the driver in a Creole that I believed to be typically Haitian. He seemed to be watching my bag with great interest. As he tried to go in another direction, I showed him the normal route; He immediately complied and, after a few minutes, dropped me off safe and sound in front of the hospital.

When I entered the room occupied by Jacques, I noticed the presence of his sister, Raymonde. The size of my mysterious bag aroused their curiosity. I immediately poured the contents of the singular on the bed, exclaiming: "Jacques, here is the money for your arm!" I must admit here that I have such a trying memory of that moment that at the precise moment when I violently put down the exclamation mark at the end of the previous sentence, the light on my work table went out.

The sight of all this money left me speechless. As their silence continued, I made these very concrete remarks to wake them up. "You, Raymonde, help Jacques count the money owed to each of the doctors and the hospital administration. To achieve this, all you have to do is consult the invoices that have been presented to us. »

A little later, I phoned the doctors to invite them to meet with us that evening to settle our various scores. According to my instructions, Jacques had prepared in small denominations the amount to be given to the doctors, to facilitate the counting operation. I had previously made arrangements to pay the administration's bill. In short, everything was done in order. Jacques' young auxiliary driver came to pick us up in our van; I gave him a gift of money, as well as to Jacques' sister, We dropped her off at her house, after which I gave the young man leave. Having then gotten behind the wheel of the van, I returned with Jacques to my niece's house.

When we arrived, a strong surprise awaited us. The courtyard of the property was all illuminated. Yolaine had decorated, for Christmas, the outside of the house as well as the garden. The overall view seemed magical. However, after I had opened the great gate, we could not enter, the house being locked. The servant was absent, as was the court boy. It was then ten o'clock in the evening. We had to wait outside. At least we were no longer cooped up in the hospital. I then began to remember all my actions and emotions of the last few days.

At first, I felt relieved that I had persevered and achieved my goal, and I thanked God for that. I had a thought of gratitude for my sister Claire and her husband Gosling: it was, of course, thanks to their exemplary corporation that I managed to sell the land and raise the amount I urgently needed. Only, I don't remember that Jacques never expressed his gratitude to them, or me, for that matter.

Throughout this adventure, I acted like a robot. And my nerves have only cracked once; it was the third evening after the accident, when Jacques had just been hospitalized. The young boy had dropped me off at my niece's house and left to come back to pick me up the next day. I did not eat the supper that the servant had prepared for me. I felt deeply sad, and I was absorbed in dark thoughts. I must point out here that during the second night, I slept in the hospital. Despite my intense grief and the circumstances of his accident, he had insisted on making love. I finally gave in, even though I found his attitude unseemly: But at the same time, I made the decision not to sleep in the hospital anymore.

All this had happened, I felt, because Jacques had never agreed to listen to any of my advice. In a fit of anger, I told my niece and her husband that I intended to return to Montreal immediately and alone. I would notify Jacques' family, who would then have no choice but to take care of him. As for me, Jacques had become irredeemable. All his past actions confirmed this. In any case, he swore that he would rather die in Haiti than return to Montreal. It was only after realizing that none of his loved ones cared about his health that he resigned himself to returning to Canada

Seeing how exhausted I was, my niece's husband advised me to go to sleep. "The night will bring you advice," he added. You'll make your decision tomorrow. They went to bed, and so did I. I couldn't pray anymore. All this happened two days after the accident. And I hadn't been to Miragoane yet. That night, I didn't sleep at all. I cried all the tears in my body. I was in so much pain inside. I felt both hatred and dejection. And probably much more.

I was choked with sobs. I called Jesus to come and help me see clearly within myself in order to make the right choice. It was 4 a.m. and I couldn't fall asleep yet. In the end, I just dozed off around 5:30 a.m. And when I woke up at 6 a.m., I got the answer. I should continue. I couldn't leave Jacques in the hands of my family. I had to go all the way. If I went back to Montreal, I had to take him with me.

I immediately told my niece. I let him know that I intended to do my best to find the money for the trip to bring Jacques back to Montreal. As a Canadian citizen in Montreal, he would be entitled to good care. I'll see what happens next. I thanked all these people for their precious support.

So far, many people who know my story have told me that if they were me, they would have left Jacques in Haiti. Given my extreme sensitivity, it would have been impossible for me to do so. In all my life, I would have regretted my action. I admit, he didn't deserve me to suffer so much for him. My suffering would be even more excruciating, however, to know that he is suffering a long martyrdom and that I have left him there without help.

"Blessed are the merciful, for they will obtain mercy. Jerusalem Bible, Luke 6:36-39. »

Part Four

A Christmas Night Under the Stars, 1996

That evening, when I left the hospital, I went to a pharmacy. I bought the pain medication and antibiotics that the doctors had prescribed for Jacques.

Since there was no one at home, I put Jacques in a rocking chair that was on the porch. Having put on some clothes that were in my suitcase, I remained seated in the van.

It was a full moon night, the Christmas lights were twinkling, and it was magical. I felt relaxed. I was calm and confident. It was as if I was surrounded by angels. I felt protected. I felt happiness in my heart. I didn't see the time passing. I wasn't sleeping because I wasn't sleepy.

At midnight, I went to see Jacques on the porch. He was asleep, and I didn't want to disturb him. I took a few steps in front of the house. I looked at the sky in its fullness, as well as the moon and the stars. I could hear music in my head. I started thinking about my children and my family in Montreal. But in a good way, because I saw them happy and I was delighted.

I got back in the van and prayed to God, thanking Him for all His kindness. Around 1 a.m., the court boy arrived. He was surprised to see us in the courtyard. He told me that no one expected Jacques to leave the hospital the night before. He told us that the occupants of the house had left for a New Year's Eve party. He put us in the servant's room, not having the key to the big house. I put Jacques to bed in the maid's little bed, and I sat in a chair all the rest of the night. Thanks to the medication, Jacques was able to sleep.

At around 5:30 a.m., I went out into the yard and noticed that Dane's car was there. I went to knock on the window of the room. He came to open the door for me. He thought I had just arrived. I told her that we had been here a long time ago and that we had spent the night in the maid's room. As they seemed very sorry about this, I reassured them by explaining that I was the one who had accelerated the events with the help of Jesus and the family in Miragoâne, since I did not want to spend Christmas in the hospital with Jacques. I told them that we would leave on December 26 because Jacques could not keep his arm in plaster any longer.

On December 25, at 12:30 p.m., I called Air Canada in Haiti to make the reservations. It was anxious that the tickets should be paid immediately. Dany took me to the Air Canada counter to do it, and while at home, Jacques, with his sick arm, helped by the court boy, tried to repair our big refrigerator. He was planning to sell it to a friend of my niece. He had to repair it at the cost of intense pain in his arm. When I got home, I started packing. The next morning, everything was ready for departure.

When we arrived at the airport, I administered a powerful medication to Jacques to reduce the violent throbbing of his arm and the smell that was beginning to emerge from it. He slept a little on the plane. The trip could not have been more difficult, despite the fact that we were seated in first class. This was how Jacques, in spite of his fierce obstinacy. Was forced to leave Haitian soil

Chapter 5

Emergency return to Montreal, Thursday, December 26, 1997
Part One

Jacques ends up at Notre-Dame Hospital

Natatsha and Patrick picked us up at the Montreal airport, Jacques being of course in a wheelchair when he arrived in Montreal, they came to pick him up in a wheelchair. They took us directly to the emergency room of Notre-Dame Hospital. The day before, Natatsha had taken care to warn Jacques' doctor of our arrival, who had informed the hospital. As soon as we arrived, Jacques was put in a room in the emergency room, and a doctor came to examine him. I gave him the file that the surgeon had given me. He asked me for some further explanations. Then it was time for first aid.

As Jacques is diabetic and had hardly eaten, he was first given serum. Realizing that he was in good hands, I went to find Natatsha and Patrick while thinking about taking a good shower as soon as possible and then resting in a comfortable bed. Another decisive step had just ended. I felt relieved. Jacques was being treated in a hospital in Montreal. I said thank you to God.

Present Moment, November 29, 2006

At noon, I take a break. I'm exhausted. Too many painful memories. It is midnight. I wrote for six hours. My neck and back hurt.

Present Moment, December 6, 2006

1:15 p.m. *Since November 29, 2006, I have not written anything. At first, it was because the part I had just written had completely exhausted me psychologically. I wanted to clear my mind before continuing. But in addition, I was getting ready to receive my little family on Sunday, December 3rd, on the occasion of Christmas. Taking advantage of little Elle-Camay's birthday, I organized a delicious supper for both this birthday and the commemoration of the birth of Christ.*

My desire to focus on my writing activity was unfortunately thwarted by a silly accident that, on December 4th, my daughter and I had on the Decarie Expressway. The van was heavily damaged. For my daughter, it was a severe emotional shock, followed by pain in my neck. As for me, as I had already suffered three hard accidents, my body was badly bruised.

Today, I will nevertheless try to continue my writing project. Maybe I'll get back to it tonight...

In the hospital: back to my story

When I joined Natatsha in the hospital waiting room, she told me that she would take me to Rosita, a cousin of Jacques' who lived in Montreal North. She had made these arrangements because, for the moment, she and her little family were staying with Patrick's mother in Repentigny. She was waiting to move soon to her own house that she and her husband had just bought.

It turned out that I couldn't go to my sister's house because of the fact that I had gone back to live with Jacques. On the other hand, I felt that Montreal North was a long way from the hospital. But I was so tired that I couldn't question anything anymore

My daughter and her husband dropped me off at Rosita's house. She put her bedroom at my disposal. All in all, I was well received. She had prepared food for me. I started by taking a good shower, then I ate while conversing with Rosita. She wanted me to tell her about the accident, which I did. Immediately after, I went upstairs to rest in the room. I was finally in Montreal in a very welcoming and comfortable room. I slept in one go. I badly needed it. I felt very calm for the first time since the accident. My mind was at peace.

The next day, at 8 a.m., I used public transport to get to Notre-Dame Hospital. I found the journey long and exhausting. I had to take two buses and the metro. I thought of asking my friend Laura, who was living at the time on Clark Street, not far from Bernard Street, if I could come and stay with her temporarily, before renting an apartment, in anticipation of Jacques' release from the hospital. I couldn't see myself going to live with anyone with him. Not even in my children's homes.

That morning, several doctors were still examining Jacques in a room in the emergency room of a hospital center. They asked me to describe the circumstances of the accident. They couldn't figure out what kind of intervention the doctors in Haiti had applied to him. The wound on Jacques' arm gave off an unbearable smell. They decided to operate on him that morning, to remove the cast; after which, they would know what to do. I had to sign a document that allowed the doctor to amputate the arm in case they couldn't save it. A doctor advised me to pray while inviting me to go to the waiting room and warning me that the operation would be long. A few minutes later, Jacques was taken to the operating room.

In the meantime, I had called the children to tell them the news. They promised to come and keep me company towards the end of the afternoon. I phoned my sister Irene and my brother

Robert to announce that I had returned to Montreal and that Jacques was hospitalized. Actually, very brief was my phone call.

During the operation, the young doctor came back to talk to me, with tears in her eyes. "We are not finished, but I would like to know if Haiti is a country of barbarians," she added. How can a doctor send us a patient in such a state? She added, "If he had stayed one more day in Haiti, he would have died; The wound was rotting. »

She tried to calm me down by assuring me that she and her colleagues would try everything. "He must expect to suffer for some time, because we have not closed the wound," she said. Bandages will be applied twice a day for two weeks to drain the wound before the operation. He suffered several fractures to his arm and wrist. I thanked her for coming to comfort me, and she went back to the operating room.

Dinner time had arrived, but I stayed put, not too far from the operating room. At 1 p.m., the doctors finished. They kept him under observation in an intensive care room, waiting to transfer him to another room. Around 4 p.m., he was installed in a semi-private room. He looked extremely tired. But he pretended that he did not feel great pain. A doctor came to explain the procedures to me. He revealed to me that the wrist was broken into small pieces.

The arm and forearm were severed into three pieces; The elbow was also broken, and the wound had remained open and had a lot of debris. Following the two-week dressing change, specialists would evaluate the different options. He then warned Jacques: "If you are in too much pain, ask the nurses on duty for medication." Then he left, wishing us good luck and recommending that we be patient.

The first day was quiet. Jacques was still under the effects of medication. I called the children to ask them to come and see the next day, Saturday, December 28. I felt that we were both much too tired.

I then phoned my friend Laura to ask her if she could host me for a few days at her home. She agreed. I warned Jacques' cousin that I would go and stay with my friend because the journey from her home to the hospital was too long and tiring for me. She thought my decision made a lot of sense. I prepared my belongings and the next day, Patrick helped me transport them to Laura's house, after which he drove me to the hospital.

Since my arrival in Montreal, I was often shaken by chills. I really didn't feel good. I talked to Laura about it. According to her, my condition was the consequence of excessive tension. For three days, every morning, she would make me have a small cup of black coffee with salt. This treatment really did me good. My chills were gone.

At the hospital, the situation began to change. Max, Natatsha, Patrick and little Elle-Camay came to see us. I will never forget that look of Elle-Camay. She was six months old and sitting in her stroller. I went to drive them back to the elevator. Natatsha kept telling me not to tire myself too much for her father and to think of myself first. She and Max had come to the hospital to see me, she told me. She felt that Jacques had made me suffer too much. As I entered the elevator, little Elle-Camay looked at me with a smile that meant a lot of things. She held my hand for a long time. In his eyes, I thought I saw the face of an angel. And this look comforted me, while giving me more courage at the thought of the trials I still had to overcome.

During the two weeks that the nurses came to bandage Jacques' arm, I experienced extremely trying moments. With each bandage, it was hell. Jacques was in so much pain that he lost consciousness. For my part, I couldn't look at the wound. The sight was too horrible. I was in a lot of pain every time, and my heart was tortured.

One day, one of the nurses was absent, so the one who was doing the bandage at the time asked me to help her hold Jacques' arm. When I saw the wound, I almost lost consciousness. While I held the arm, the nurse removed the bandage, cleaned the wound, and applied a new bandage. This stage was the most unbearable. The wound was open from the top of to arm up to the wrist; it was spread out like a piece of meat that was cut into small pieces for cooking. It was disgusting and excruciating, and I felt all the pain myself. He turned his eyes away from the wound. I remember well that he never looked at her until she was completely healed.

As I write these lines, I am once again experiencing all the suffering of those moments. My heart hurts so much. In addition to my pain, I had to support Jacques morally, given his persistent bad mood. I was very unhappy. He absolutely did not want anyone to come and visit him. If anyone ever showed up, they pretended to be asleep.

For my part, I did everything I could to make sure that his anger did not show. The nurses thought he was obnoxious to me because of the way he spoke to me.

On New Year's Day, when it was time to put on the bandage, I was in so much pain that I needed to talk to someone to feel human warmth. I just wanted a little attention; I phoned my children. No answer. I resigned myself to calling my sister Irene. She answered me very coldly. I confessed to her how sad I was and how much I suffered: "It's your business," she replied dryly, "it's you who chose it." I could hear the voices of people talking in the background. She received her friends. I expressed the wish to speak to Vivianne. When she picked up the phone, she said: "Ah! It's you, Enice, we're celebrating," laughing. I wished him a happy New Year, and I hung up my phone right away.

Retrospective of the progress

I found myself alone in this story and got out of it alone too. I went to the hospital chapel to seek comfort in prayer. Now I understand the attitude of all these people towards me. It was really me who got myself into this mess, Irene was right to react as she did. They had witnessed the undignified treatment this man had inflicted on me. They didn't understand why I agreed to support him to such an extent. But what do you want? I did it. I didn't regret it. All in all, I think I saved a life. Period, that's all.

Part Two

The operation of Jacques' arm

Fifteen days after the dressing treatment, on January 10, 1998, a doctor came to tell us that the operation was scheduled for the next day at around 10 a.m. and that Jacques had to be fasting. We were relieved. Finally, no more bandages. The next morning, Jacques was ready. He was waiting for someone to pick him up and take him to the operating room. It was noon, and Jacques was still in the room. Around 1 p.m., a nurse pointed out to me that there were other patients who needed to be operated on. It would be at 4 p.m. In the end, we spent all day and night waiting. I had to sleep in the hospital.

On the morning of January 12, Jacques asked me to go and get him a wheelchair and put him in it. He had decided to go see the nurse in charge himself because he thought I was too nice to the staff.

He went to the guard station in a wheelchair. Calling out to the nurse, he asked to contact the doctor. The nurse tried to convince him that the wheelchair was not suitable for his condition and that he should stay down. He turned a deaf ear. He stormed, "If I have to, I'll stay here at the post until the operation takes place."

Weary of war, the nurse called the doctor, who confirmed that Jacques would be the first to have the operation at 8:30 a.m.

The nurse and I helped him to bed. At the appointed time, at 8:30 a.m., we came to pick him up. I took the opportunity to go to lunch in the cafeteria. I made a little toilet in the room. The operation lasted six hours.

Jacques was brought back to the room at 3:30 p.m. His arm was in plaster up to his fingers. He was not in a good mood. He didn't speak. An hour later, he wanted to urinate. I presented him with the potty, "No! he yelled, I want to go urinate in the toilet. I kept telling him that the doctor had recommended that he not get up. He yelled, "I have nothing to do with the doctor! Take me to the bathroom right now! I left the room to get the nurse.

The nurse confirmed my words. Jacques wanted nothing to do with it. He wanted to throw himself out of bed. The nurse went to get a wheelchair. She warned me that if an accident occurred, she would not be responsible for it. I painfully helped him get out of bed, and he sat down in the wheelchair. In the bathroom, it was also difficult for me to set it up so that I could pee. I couldn't take it anymore. I was exhausted. I had been up for more than 24 hours.

During Jacques' hospitalization, I thought every day about the need to rent an apartment. Since I didn't own a car, I had to find one not far from the hospital. In this connection, I relate the following curious incident.

At one point, I had asked Max to come and visit the apartments with me. One day, I had made an appointment with him near the Mont-Royal metro station. I was walking down the street and talking to myself. I passed Max without even seeing him. He touched me and whispered: "Mammy, it's me, Max, don't you recognize me?" I said, "Oh yes, that's you, Max."

Things were going very badly for me. It was almost the end of January. It was cold. It often snowed. I felt like a madwoman. We had to find the apartment as quickly as possible, because Jacques was going to leave the hospital soon. Max and I went to visit an apartment. It was a 1 1/2. He was so dirty. Max pointed out to me that I couldn't live there at all. The building also smelled of drugs. A little discouraged, I went back to the Jacques hospital to be released in three days. I asked the doctor for a week. For the search for the apartment. He granted it to me.

I went to the hospital mainly to give Jacques his bath. I didn't stay there all day because of his almost constant bad mood. But he still wanted us to have sex every time I gave him his bath. I tried to make him understand that the only concern at the moment was the rental of an apartment. I was at the end of these incessant movements. My resistance only fueled his anger.

When I told him of my pressing concern, he suggested that I contact the person in charge of the building where he lived, on Port-Royal Street near Saint-Laurent Street. I immediately followed his advice. Fortunately, there were 2 1/2 furnished apartments.

I went there the next day. The building was very clean and had a permanent surveillance office and an elevator. The person in charge showed me around an apartment on the third floor. The lease was monthly, which suited me perfectly. I told him that I was taking the apartment, but I was planning to replace the mattress. Before going to the hospital, I went to buy a mattress. We were supposed to deliver it in two days.

As soon as I returned to the hospital, I told Jacques the news. I then notified the hospital. The next morning, when the doctor came in for his visit, I informed him that I had found an apartment. He announced that Jacques would be discharged the next day. He was supposed to come back in 30 days for checks. The health professional prescribed pain medication.

I had called the children to provide them with the address of the apartment. I took the opportunity to ask Patrick to pick us up the next day at the hospital around 11 a.m. On the appointed day, we took possession of the apartment. But Jacques seemed very dissatisfied at the time. The employee who came to deliver the mattress to us pointed out the fact, while urging me to be vigilant: "Madam, be careful, the gentleman is very angry; He keeps yelling at you. I tried to reassure him: "Don't worry about me: if he's in a bad mood," I said, "it's because his arm still hurts."

I felt strange in this apartment as well as in the neighborhood. There was no one in the streets. It was not a strictly residential area. It consisted mainly of office buildings and factories. Port-Royal Street intersects Saint-Laurent Street. I promised myself that I wouldn't stay there very long, just so I could have peace of mind.

The apartment had a bedroom that could accommodate a double bed and a bathroom. The room was separated by a screen from the small living room and the small kitchen. A fairly large window opened onto the back balcony. In the small kitchen, a small table and two chairs. A small two-plate cooker, a small refrigerator. A three-seater sofa. A wardrobe, a desk in the bedroom, and the bed. This was our little apartment of suffering and misery.

During Jacques' hospitalization, Natatsha told me that she was pregnant with a second child. At the time, I didn't know what to say to him because I had too many of my problems.

Chapter 6

Life together on Port-Royal Street

Living with James in a 2 1/2

The first night, Jacques suffered a lot. He did not have sufficient pain medication. For my part, I didn't have time to buy him anything else. The next morning, I walked along Sauvé Street in the cold while wishing to decline a pharmacy nearby. To my great disappointment, there were none. I came back empty-handed. My daughter, to whom I confided in my distress, reminded me that by dialing 411, I would get the contact details of a pharmacy near my home. Which I did immediately. Very quickly, the medicines were delivered to me. My friend Laura, for her part, brought me bags of food products. She pointed out to me the existence of a food market on Rue Sauvé; I could, she told me, walk there.

During the whole time I stayed in this apartment, it was in this, commonly known as the "Sauvé Market," that I made my orders. In the meantime, I was experiencing all the miseries in the world with Jacques. Every day, I bathed him, and I had to do everything for him since he could not use his arm; The whole thing became exceedingly arduous, the plaster making an arc with a stick that held the arm in place. His condition made him so angry that he demolished his personal belongings, such as his video camera and his tape recorder.

The children came to see us on weekends, but Jacques didn't want any visitors. At night, I didn't sleep much because he was constantly moving, and he constantly wanted to make love despite his pain; it helped him sleep, he assured me. My morale was at its lowest. But I didn't let Jacques notice my state of depression. He must not have seen me crying. It was in the middle of the street that I was going to shed my tears. I would occasionally take refuge in a passage that connected Sauvé Street and Port-Royal Street. When I went to do my shopping at the Sauvé Market, I was moving in the snow and I was screaming very loudly. My screams relieved me.

At the same time, I called on Jesus for help. My sobs redoubled. I couldn't control myself anymore. In any case, I was a little crazy. The creditors began to harass us. Once and for all, Jacques said to one of them: "I explained my case to you and you say you want money! Well, my dear friend comes, I will wait for you with my gun!" and hung up. The man's boss called for clarification. Jacques told him about his accident and told him that he was receiving social assistance. His interlocutor was very understanding. He advised us to sign up for the "voluntary deposit" program, and he described the procedures for it.

The time had come to show up for the hospital appointment. We went there by taxi. The doctor removed the cast. He was satisfied with his work. He put on other bandages in addition to a bandage to hold the arm and protect it. He recommended us to the nearest CLSC for the following dressings and ordered us to come back in a week to remove the braces from the wrist.

It had become even more tiring to take public transit every day for bandages. I asked the nurse in charge of the CLSC if she could send a caregiver to our home because all these trips were exhausting for Jacques. As it was also very cold, he could not fit his arm into the sleeve of his coat. A nurse showed up. She pointed out to me that from the data in my file, I could do the dressings myself. She would show me how to go about it and provide me with everything I needed. I was clearly not in a position to refuse. So, I was caught up changing the bandage every day, watching that arm heal, day after day, until the wound was completely closed, having to endure Jacques' suffering during each bandage and giving him his bath. I was physically and morally depressed.

He was getting calmer, but I was almost psychologically demolished. Exhausted, I no longer had control of my mind. The braces on the wrist having been removed and the wound closed, he could take his bath alone; He also started going out to run errands on his own. I called my adoptive mother. I told her that I was physically and mentally exhausted. Could she recommend a place with the nuns where I would stay for a few days? She recommended me. "The Franciscan Missionary Sisters of Mary." Sur at Laurier Street, at the corner of Colonial Street.

I made a reservation by phone for the following week. Five days before, I told Jacques that I was going to stay with the nuns to rest for a while. In the meantime, his cousin Rosita gladly agreed to take him in.

He tried to hold me back. I told him that I couldn't even think anymore. I felt the painful feeling of having lost my mind. At night, I didn't sleep anymore. I cried in secret. He finally whispered to me, "If this is what will make you feel good, then go for it." I told the owner of the building that I would leave the following week. I packed my suitcases and Jacques' suitcases. I left the place a day before him. I felt unhappy to leave him, but I was really at the end of my strength and nerves. So, that's how I abandoned the apartment in Port-Royal (and left Jacques for a third time).

After I left, I couldn't stand being told about the accident, and especially about Jacques' arm. Each time, my stomach hurt. I was marked by this event for a long time. I could no longer drive in the heights, or if I was in a car, when we went down a slope, I closed my eyes. As for Jacques' arm, since the last bandage, I have never looked at it again. He reminded me too much of my atrocious sufferings. All because of this man's stubbornness. If he had listened to me when I strongly recommended that he return the truck to its owner, such a misfortune would not have happened. But it was done. If the same opportunity presented itself, I would act quite differently.

Chapter 7

Among the nuns

My stay with the nuns

When I arrived at the nuns' home, I was greeted by a sister who helped me bring my luggage to a room. She gave me the key to this room and showed me around the whole floor. At the same time, she showed me the location of the toilets and bathrooms. We then went down to the ground floor where the refectory, the chapel, and the waiting room were located. The sister then took me to the principal's office, where I then wrote down my name and paid the month's rent. The director gave me the instructions of the convent. When I left her office, I went to the chapel to pray to God and ask for His help.

Back in the room that had been reserved for me, I put my things away; Then I called my children to tell them where I was. This seemed to reassure them. Natatsha recommended that I take care of myself.

I felt really good in this place. Wanting peace at all costs. I hadn't given Jacques my contact details. Having completely lost my points of reference, I had a pressing need to see clearly within myself. A calm, serene place bathed in spirituality became essential to me.

I called my sister to tell her that I had just left Jacques and that I was staying with the nuns on Laurier Street. I gave him the address. I didn't have a phone in my room yet. A common telephone was installed in the corridor. At the beginning of my stay, I slept a lot. Every morning, I went to Mass in the chapel and returned to say my evening prayers. I badly needed it. It was spring and my daughter was pregnant with her second child. Occasionally, she would come to see me. I would go for short walks with her. Slowly, I began to come to my senses again. I had resumed therapy. The treatment was good for me. I walked the way, which allowed me to meditate while walking and exercise.

I soon had a phone installed in my room. Only my sister and my children had the number. One day, an intercom call tells me that someone on the phone insists on talking to me. It was Jacques. He told me that he had called several times and that the sisters always replied that I was absent. This time, he had pretended to be my brother. He stammered that it was his cousin who had given him the number of my retirement self. He asked me to meet with him about some car insurance papers I had to sign. I promised him that I would call him to tell him about my decision.

I tried to avoid seeing him again so soon because I still felt very vulnerable. In addition, my full health had not returned. I had experienced so much suffering because of this man.

A few days later, however, I phoned him to set up an appointment at a location I had chosen myself. The meeting had been scheduled for April 26, 1997, at a café located at the corner of Saint-Laurent and Rachel streets. I had prayed before I left and I felt strong and confident. I didn't feel any emotion during our interview. He kept telling me that he thought a lot about me and that he still loved me. I tried to make him understand that for the moment, I wasn't in the mood for romantic relationships. I promised him that he would have my decision soon. We didn't stay in the café for long, only about thirty minutes. When I returned to the boarding house, I felt proud of myself, and at the same time, I thought that I had to tell him very firmly that I no longer intended to live with him, so that he would have no hope of a possible return.

The next day was Saturday, April 27, 1997. It was on that day that I seriously decided to start writing my first book. Here is what I wrote in my diary.

Here are some parts of my diary, during my stay with the nuns on Laurier Street in Montreal. From the end of April to the end of May.

27 April 1997 - Journal

On this beautiful spring Saturday, I woke up very early while thinking about yesterday when I met Jacques at the restaurant not far from the convent where I had been living for a month. I had to leave it to come and spend a few months in this house, in order to think of myself and regain my inner peace.

I was depressed. Since Jacques's accident, he had become very aggressive and bitter towards me again. However, I was the one who took care of him. I needed to think and find myself. To achieve this, I had to take refuge in a quiet, welcoming place that was conducive to meditation. I especially wanted to know who I really was and to take stock of how my life has gone over the past year.

Because I don't feel at peace, it seems to me that there is a part of me that I ignore and that prevents me from moving forward normally. I have to get to know her to be able to really be me. It is also for this reason that I came to live for a while in the convent. I felt a need to get closer to God. I wanted to be close to him. To get there, I had to get away from my family and my husband Jacques.

I was happy because I was going to be able to start writing, but I didn't know when. First of all, I had to find a way to get rid of Jacques. So, I decided to submit my decision to break up to him in writing, so that he would know that there was nothing left between us. A part of me resisted this idea a little; I had to force myself to perform the gesture at all costs.

At the restaurant, I told him that I didn't love him anymore so that he could give me back my freedom. A very difficult feeling to express, but it was better for me. I think it was also painful for him to hear such words come out of my mouth. After making such a decision that morning, I had a feeling that it would not be a day like any other.

I went downstairs to lunch and attended mass. I thanked God for giving me back my courage and also for all that He had done for me.

I continue my story
Monday, 11 December 2006

Despite my momentous expressions of faith, I could not recover my health. I had anxiety attacks, and I always had stomach pain. To the point that I had to consult a doctor. After several examinations, I learned that my illness was not directly medical. I'm anxious. I continued to write in my journal, but I couldn't continue writing my book. I was plagued by anxiety. Yet I was filled with affection from my children and my sister.

Monday, May 12, 1997 — Journal

I am back at the convent. I'm in my room on the third floor. I feel depressed. I shouldn't be like this, because yesterday I had my best Mother's Day since I became a mother. My children have spoiled me. I was amazed. It was the best gift I've ever had. They did it themselves. This is one of my photos, then I was 22 years old, which Natatsha reproduced in a drawing, accompanied by beautiful poems written by her and Max. They framed it, and Max gave me a brooch that represented a giraffe. I was very happy with these gifts. I thanked them with hugs.

Let's go back to today and the subject of my depressive state. Today, I don't know if it's because of the temperature, because it's been raining since yesterday evening. I can't write anything. I think I'll take a little nap, then I'll probably be fine.

Tuesday, May 13, 1997 — Journal

I reflected on why I was depressed yesterday. It's because I had a stormy argument with Jacques on the phone. It brought back bad memories for me. I talked to Monique, the therapist. She confirmed that this was indeed the cause of my depression.

I walked a lot today; it did me good. My sister Irene has just returned from a trip to Florida. She told me about her time there and about a friend who was sick. I listened carefully to what he said, but it left me indifferent. I had suffered so much, now I was starting to get out of it. At times, I felt insensitive to others. God forgive me, that was the way it was. But for my family, it's not the same. These days, I am very worried about my daughter because of her pregnancy.

Wednesday, May 14, 1997 — Journal

This morning, I woke up at 7:45 a.m. For me, it was a bit late. I didn't have a good night. I had a lot of nightmares that I don't even remember. I went to mass. My sister Irene called me to talk to me again about a friend's illness in Florida and other topics that did not concern me. It's sad for people, but what could I do for them in the state I was in?

I went to the swimming pool. Then I went to dinner. Back in my room, I felt anxious again. I scolded myself: "Enice, pull yourself together, you have good books to read, you can draw, and also you can write. Because you have so many things to tell!

So, I started writing about my childhood, about my mother's death. When the phone rang, it was my sister Irene who was calling me. I was deep into the events surrounding my mother's death, to the point where I jumped at the phone ringing. My sister asked me what I was doing. I told him that I was writing. Noticing that I was preoccupied, she whispered to me: I'll leave you. I'll call you back, and hung up immediately.

I then stopped writing. I couldn't go on. Instead, I started drawing. After dinner, I sat down at my desk to read a very interesting book: In the Name of All Mine, by author Martin Gray. Around 7 p.m., my sister called me to tell me that she would come to see me at 8 p.m. When she arrived, she invited me to accompany her to a small tea room called Kilo on Saint-Laurent Street, for tea and cake. I enjoyed a nice piece of three-fruit cheesecake, my favorite, and she chose one with strawberries. We stayed for an hour talking about everything and nothing. Not a word about Jacques. I was happy with my evening, too. She then dropped me off at the convent and continued on foot.

It was 10:30 p.m. Thirty minutes later, I phoned my sister's house to check that she had arrived. I got ready to sleep. My daughter called me to confirm our appointment the next day, because I had to go with her to her medical appointment, for the follow-up of her pregnancy. It was seven months old.

Friday, December 15 — Journal

I spent a wonderful month of May at the convent. Since Natatsha was not doing well during her pregnancy, I went to see her very often. And sometimes I would stay in bed at her house when her husband worked late at night. The doctor had recommended that we watch her because, he told us, the child was not doing well.

Despite all this, I continued to go to therapy. The treatment was good for me. I couldn't write and at the same time go out with my sister as often as I used to. With all this back and forth, I felt very tired. At least I didn't have to answer to anyone. I remember one morning, I felt very determined. I wanted to really change, to be completely autonomous.

Here's what I wrote that morning in my diary

Friday, May 22, 1997 — Diary

I'm standing. I look at the painting that my children gave me for Mother's Day. I start talking to Enice about the portrait: "Enice at the age of 22. Young, fresh, innocent, sensitive, but strong and optimistic. For 30 years, I let myself be crushed and humiliated by two men, Tony and Jacques. Now that my daughter and son have recreated you, don't let anyone flatten you anymore. After talking to my portrait, I start talking to myself: "I, Enice, in the present, want to be like in the past, ready to go for it. I want to be someone for myself. I want to think about myself. I want to be autonomous. I want to work for money to help battered and humiliated women. I want to go out whenever I want. Traveling, seeing other countries and other people. I don't like to be locked up. I feel that I can. »

I gave myself the goal that one day I would be proud of myself. I don't need others to be proud of me. I'll do all of this just for myself. For my children, I am already proud of them, and I thank God for everything, and I know that He will help me achieve my goal. I really appreciated that my daughter had recreated me with the help of my son and that they had written these beautiful poems in my honor. I thank them for that.

Tales of a multifaced life written by Enice Toussaint.

It is the third Volume of four Volumes published by ENS Publishing

Éditions Nouveau Siècle.

For information, contact Natatsha Casimir

Visit our website: www.enspublishing.com

Email: ediontionsens@gmail.com

www.ingramcontent.com/pod-product-compliance
Lightning Source LLC
Chambersburg PA
CBHW061231070526
44584CB00030B/4080